Shannon!

All the very best

A leader of leaders, John Wilson and CEO Global Network drive accountability into the corner office.

Glenn Laverty, President and CEO, Ricoh Canada Inc.

John Wilson and CEO Global Network provide me with real opportunities to improve my leadership capabilities. They give me, and all CEO Global Network members, an effective sounding board, an exceptional learning environment, and most importantly, a clear and distortion-free mirror.

David Dobbin, Former President and CEO, Mobilicity

John Wilson defines contagious leadership. In over 25 years of business leadership, I have never met a person who lives, breathes, and spreads continuous self-improvement and best practices like John. His endless energy and passion know no bounds, and all he touch become better leaders and people for having John in their lives.

Graham Clark, President, Total Power Ltd.

I am a better manager and leader as a result of joining CEO Global Network. And my enthusiasm for CEO Global Network and my commitment to my CEO Group are renewed every time I meet John Wilson in person. John's passion for what he does is infectious.

Clifford Sarjeant, President and CEO, NCI Canada Inc.

John Wilson convinced me that by joining CEO Global Network I would be empowered and enabled to grow the company to the level I had dreamed about. *Not only did we do that, but the company has actually quadrupled in size. The input I receive from my fellow CEO Global Network Group members gives me the confidence to tackle any problem or opportunity that may arise in my business. I know what's happening on a minute-by-minute basis and can react to changes before they become surprises.*

Bill Kooy, Owner, Kooy Brothers Equipment Ltd.

John Wilson just gets it! His vision, mentoring, and approach to people are part of his fabric.

Chris Powell, Vice President, Sales, Tree of Life Canada ULC

CEO Global Network and its leader, John Wilson, have had a profound impact on my performance at work. The peer group, educational, and personal support I receive have improved my quality of life and our company's shareholder value. What else can you ask for from a CEO organization? John is a one-of-a-kind leader who "keeps my saw sharp."

Anne Martin, CEO, United Van Lines

John Wilson is an inspirational leader who is passionately focused on improving the lives of anyone he comes in contact with. To spend time with John is a privilege.

Chris Gower, Executive Vice President, PCL Constructors Canada Inc.

Working with John Wilson these past 10 years has had a profound impact on my business and personal life balance. It has taught me that my company is there to serve me; I do not serve my company.

My monthly meetings with my CEO Global Network Group are a sanctuary where I can be completely open with my successes, my mistakes, my failures, and my fears, knowing that everything discussed with my Group will remain behind closed doors. Our Group is dedicated to helping each other become better CEOs, better leaders, and achieve a better business–personal life balance.

We all lead very busy lives and time is at a premium, yet I do not miss my CEO Global Network Group meeting.

Steve Hartman, P.Eng., Chairman and CEO, Industrial Thermo Polymers Ltd.

From the first meeting when I met John more than a decade ago, my life has certainly been enriched. John's vision for helping CEOs achieve greater levels of success both personally and professionally is exactly what I've needed over these years.

Dean Martin, Owner, Melmart Distributors Inc.

Over the past eight years John has been a great mentor and friend to me. His crusade to make CEOs better for themselves, their families, and their companies is sincere. I don't think I have met an individual more passionate about mak-

ing a difference than John. He really keeps your "feet to the fire" to get the job done, but always in a respectful, friendly manner.

Dale I. Findlay, Former Vice President and General Manager, NCI Canada

John Wilson is the most passionate guy I have met when it comes to helping people succeed in business.

The learning opportunities I have had, and the safe haven I have enjoyed being a member of one of John's CEO Groups for close to 10 years, are experiences I would not trade for any other business learning I have tried.

Jim Greenwood, Retired head of Gordon Food Service Canada Company Inc., and former CEO and owner of Finlay Greenwood

I joined CEO Global Network shortly after being promoted to President. John Wilson has been my mentor since, on both a personal and business level. The information and confidence gained by being part of such an organization has been transforming. Or as one of my VPs said, "Joining CEO Global Network was the best thing I ever did."

Jamie Moody, President, Tree of Life Canada ULC

John Wilson's sole focus is to help you as a CEO realize your full potential by providing within CEO Global Network an environment, the tools/resources, and teammates who are 150 percent committed to your success. What more could you ask for?

Michael Burrows, CEO, Maple Lodge Farms

JOHN WILSON

FOUNDER OF CEO GLOBAL NETWORK

with Rick Fitzgerald

GREAT
CEOs
and
HOW THEY
ARE MADE

THE SEVEN IMPERATIVES

FIRST EDITION

Library and Archives Canada Cataloguing in Publication

Wilson, John, 1941 Sept. 5-
    Great CEOs and how they are made : the seven imperatives / John
    Wilson, with Rick Fitzgerald.

Includes index.
ISBN 978-0-9918373-0-4

1. Chief executive officers. 2. Success in business.
3. Leadership. 4. Executive ability. I. Fitzgerald, Rick, 1952- II. Title.

HD38.2.W554 2013
658.4'2   C2013-900414-9

Published by CEO Global Network Publishing Inc.
131 Bloor Street West, Suite 806, Toronto, Ontario, Canada M5S 1S3

This book is available at quantity discounts for educational, business or promotional use. Please direct inquiries to sales@greatceos.com.

Printed in Canada

MIX
Paper from
responsible sources
FSC
www.fsc.org   FSC® C004071

This book is dedicated to the five people who give my life meaning beyond my expectations. My mom, dad and sister Janice. My wife Lynne and our daughter Jen.

I owe them everything...

Contents

Foreword

This book includes the very best practical methods and procedures a CEO can employ to enhance his or her business, distilled down to their very essence.

Like the author, the book gets to the point quickly without the long, rambling parables that frequently fill the pages of many of today's management books. The practical, direct and helpful nature of this book is a reflection of the author.

John Wilson exudes wisdom and personifies authenticity. In this book are the insights he has collected over years as a successful CEO in the US and Canada, and after engaging with hundreds of CEOs as a mentor.

In recent years, John has institutionalized his vision for enhancing the lives and businesses of CEOs through an extensive peer group network of business leaders. That expanding network has evolved into a diverse community of CEOs, of both large and not so large public companies and owner-operated businesses, who are lifelong learners and who celebrate best practices and authenticity in action.

As a former football player, John knows what it is to block for the runner. Not to always call the play or run with the ball, but to quickly discern the action and dive in to help. Likewise, as a CEO mentor he has identified or created a number of metrics or procedures—"Imperatives"—to help CEOs discern patterns and plot a course in real time. The take-aways from each Imperative are intuitive and ready to un-pack. Each also contains proven tools for business leaders, collected from among the very best thinkers and advisors of the last generation.

In reviewing the Seven Imperatives, you will see some frequently used words. Magic words: Engagement. Accountability. Vision. Balance. Authenticity. Emotional Intelligence. Communication. Decisiveness. Clarity of Purpose. Words loaded with meaning that for many readers will no doubt call to mind past seminars, management books and forgotten "to-do" lists.

However this book is not about detailed explanations of basic concepts. This book is not for those aspiring to their first management position. This is not "Business 101." This is grad school, and the school is, and has been, the business world. The goal here is to equip you with quick, intelligent ways to reinforce your natural desire to get out and execute.

For the CEOs who work directly with John, he is not only a coach on the sidelines; he's on the field clearing the way. For any CEO with no time-outs and loads of responsibility, this book is the next best thing to having John on the field. Tackling each Imperative in a methodical way will allow you to leverage your effectiveness so you can "work smarter." This is not a tome for your living room book-shelf. This is a guide to be kept on your desk, dog-eared and highlighted.

In this book, John summarizes his passion for CEO excellence as "noble work"—helping the few who influence the many. An underlying premise of his approach is that business is not just a zero-sum endeavor predicated on a winner take-all war of attrition. Rather, it is predicated on raising the bar for all CEOs and their companies to help unleash the creative and productive capacity of our communities. Noble work indeed.

Hugh MacKinnon, Chairman and Chief Executive Officer, Bennett Jones LLP

Preface

When the idea for this project first began to percolate, John and I quickly realized the significant value to other business leaders of a book based on what we had learned from the numerous Great CEOs we have each had the privilege of knowing and working with.

By distilling this knowledge down to the Seven Imperatives of becoming a Great CEO, we hope to have created something of lasting value for all CEOs.

As much of the book is illustrated through the individual stories of CEO Global Network Members and Group Leaders, it struck me that one story that also must be told is John Wilson's.

John is an experienced owner and builder of successful companies in both Canada and the United States and is one of the world's preeminent CEO mentors. He has demonstrated the ability to increase shareholder value and has a proven track record of building nine-figure businesses. But understanding John, his values, and what he cares about and why, is perhaps the best underpinning for this book that I can provide.

One of the things you've got to appreciate about John Wilson is that when he meets people, he quickly tries to bring them up to his high level of optimism about life. But in spite of all the wonderful things in life, life can also be very, very tough. A significant event that changed John's life forever was when his younger sister, Janice, died of cancer at the age of 14. John was 18 at the time and still has the small plastic trophy engraved "World's Best Football Player" that she gave him.

John will tell you that up until Janice's death, he had just squeaked through school, he didn't take it seriously, and got grades just high enough to move on. For John it was all about sports, and he avidly played baseball, hockey, and football.

He remembers being home one day, and, not realizing how close to death his sister actually was, he was preparing to leave for a ball game when his Dad stopped him on the stairs and said, "John, you may want to think about studying, you may want to think about your grades. Your sister is upstairs and she is very sick. You may want to take things a little more seriously."

John remembers that day like it was yesterday. And from that day forward he did take things seriously. Over the years, many wonderful things have happened in his life. But he learned the hard way that there are some defining moments when life doesn't work the way you expect it to. John knows that success is never a straight line, and life is never a straight line, and he sincerely wants to help others through the defining moments of their own lives. He has a built-in need and desire to help people become all they can be. To be there to help celebrate the victories and find strength in the tough times, because he knows from experience that they are going to come.

After receiving an MBA from the University of Western Ontario (Western University), John began a career with Ultramar Canada where he worked for 18 years, initially as VP of Sales and Marketing, and then as CEO of Ultramar Ontario Ltd., before moving to California to run a billion-dollar business as part of the Ultramar team in the United States. In 1993, soon after a company in the United Kingdom bought Ultramar, John started his own business that developed a network of fleet fueling sites across the southwestern United States. John and his partners built the business up from zero into a multimillion-dollar company.

They sold the company in 1998 and John moved his family back to Toronto in 2000. He was originally looking for a company to buy when, quite by chance, he saw an ad for executive development leaders to mentor other executives. John had belonged to a CEO development group in California, and so he contacted his former group leader who assured him that he would love it. John decided to get involved in developing their Ontario business.

He found the opportunity to help as a CEO mentor extremely fulfilling; it fit just right in his soul. John was learning a lot from the CEOs he worked with, and they often suggested ways that the sessions could be made better. But he kept hitting a brick wall when trying to implement changes, and realized he was fighting too hard to improve someone else's business. His entrepreneurial spirit kicked into gear and he decided to start his own company and create it using a model that he knew was better.

That's when he had the idea to start CEO Global Network—an organization that stands for the unmitigated success of executives, their families, and their businesses. An organization that helps people grow personally, be more successful in business, and get more time with their families. An environment where CEOs help each other succeed in business and in life. Unlike any other CEO development organization, CEO Global Network is truly committed to the success of its members by engaging the very best CEO Group Leaders, maintaining rigorous Member screening, and requiring outstanding Member commitment.

John's authentic desire to help business leaders become better at what they do and the lasting outcomes they create is impressive to say the least. Having been a member of executive learning groups, mentored by John, and having had the opportunity to lead a CEO Global Network CEO peer group, I know firsthand the impact that membership in an organization like this can have.

John Wilson passionately wants to make a positive difference in the lives of others. In creating CEO Global Network, John has made a positive difference in the lives and businesses of numerous CEOs and other leaders. In writing this book and sharing his hard-earned knowledge and insight, he is sure to help countless others.

Rick Fitzgerald

Introduction

What makes a Great CEO?

In the fall of 2010, I was asked to speak as a member of an executive panel and address the question, "What does it take to be a successful CEO in today's economy and, in your opinion, what are the top three qualities of a successful CEO?" In preparation, I reached out to a large number of CEOs for a broader view of the thinking beyond my personal perspective. I was most grateful for the numerous emails, texts, and voice messages I received in reply. The range of insights was enormous and the majority of responses centered on several key themes.

Having had the privilege of building and running successful organizations and having spent countless hours mentoring high-performing leaders, I had a pretty good idea about what it took to succeed. But in the months that followed, and in my subsequent conversations with CEOs, I began to realize that there were certain common qualities or behaviors that could be viewed as imperatives in the creation of a great business leader.

To help quantify this knowledge so that it could be shared with a larger audience, I turned to good friend and advisor Rick Fitzgerald. Rick spent hundreds of hours conducting one-on-one interviews with successful business leaders who graciously shared stories of their challenges and triumphs, and the tools they used to bridge the two on their journey to realizing success. To becoming Great.

What do I mean by Great?

Great CEOs are able to achieve success in their personal, family, and business lives. They are able to create an inspiring vision for their company, and effectively communicate that vision across their organization. They know themselves, and understand the motives and competencies of those around them. They are accountable, and know how to foster an environment of accountability. They realize the value of building and keeping a great team. They understand their numbers and can see well beyond the horizon. They get results.

How do they become Great? Great CEOs are lifelong learners. They are committed to continuous personal growth and understand that they can't do it alone. They realize that faster growth and greater success come from learning from others who have walked a similar path.

Quite often, I first meet CEOs when they have just been promoted to the corner office. To determine if we will be a good fit and how serious they are about getting on top of their game and staying there, I ask them three questions:

Question one: If you could have one decision back that you made in the past 12 months, which one is it and why do you want it back?

Most people nod their head knowingly and say, "Only one?"

But if CEOs can't answer that question; can't think of a decision they would like back; it is time to drill deeper, because everyone has one. Whether they are willing to admit it or not, no one bats a thousand. Their lack of self-awareness means I have to continue to probe. Hopefully my questions will result in a wake-up call.

Some people have more answers than questions. CEOs destined for Greatness will have more questions than answers.

Question two: What are the two biggest strategic decisions you have to make in the next year?

Listen carefully to the answer: are they working on their business or in it? Strong CEOs work on their business. They see the big picture and plan accordingly. The only person in the company with the ultimate responsibility for peering at the horizon is the CEO. Their eyes must focus on the future—where is Godzilla coming from? Where are the elephants? Where is Murphy? Where are the next big opportunities? They are out there but you can't see them with your head down.

One of the reasons CEOs fail is that they keep their eyes down and focused on the immediate task at hand. Not lifting their head up to see the big picture is a danger sign.

Question three: What is the number one thing you must get better at as the CEO of this company in order to take it to where you want to take it?

Listen carefully. What is it? What is it for you?

If the CEO can't come up with a good answer here, that indicates a big problem. Everyone can get better but not everyone is willing to admit it; not to me, not to themselves. It is a moment of truth. How well they know themselves is a crucial factor, and the ability to answer this question is critical to CEO success.

The best CEOs I work with have thoughtful answers to these three questions. They are authentic. They want to get better; sharpen the scalpel and keep it sharp.

This book is written to honor those people who take on the challenge to lead the pack, take the arrows, decide which mountain will be climbed, and who will climb it with them. Great CEOs get to the top of the mountain and then look for the next mountain to climb. These are very special people and I believe that they are made not born. Greatness is never given; it is earned! And learned!

There are of course many CEOs who have had the good fortune to be born with helpful personality traits—but while certain qualities are no doubt important to leadership, it is only through experience, learning, and development that leaders can realize their true potential and become Great.

This book is based on the CEOs I have had the privilege to know and observe, and the thousands of intense one-on-one meetings I have had with them as the founder and CEO of CEO Global Network. It is based on my experience of leading hundreds of CEO group discussions.

To paraphrase Malcolm Gladwell, it is based on my '10,000 hours.'

Throughout the book I will share with you the incredible success stories of some of the Great CEOs and entrepreneurs I have met over the past decade. One common element is that they are all members of CEO peer groups. All have an experienced mentor who is their CEO Group Leader—a seasoned CEO with a proven track record of success—to help coach and reflect with them on key challenges and opportunities. All are committed to continuous learning, personal growth, and creating the biggest possible successes for themselves, their families, and companies.

I hope that their stories will help you fast-track your own personal and business growth. I hope that by learning from them, you will significantly improve your success, your life, and the lives of those you care about.

Be clear, I am not a professional writer. I am a CEO confidant and mentor. What does that mean? It means I have had to sharply hone my ability to read between the lines. It means I have to know when to shut up and listen. It means I have enough scars and victories to ask the right questions.

It means I have to dig deep inside myself to muster up the courage to ask the questions that no one else will ask.

It means the CEOs have to know how much I care for them. Know that I stand for their success.

I have seen greatness firsthand. It quite honestly brings me to tears when I think of how fortunate I am to be with these people. Sounds corny, doesn't it? But it's true.

Why does this mean so much to me?

Because I deeply care for these people. Deeply care. Perhaps because I remember my own journey. It wasn't a straight line. I love business but it didn't always love me back. No one is going to get to the top of the mountain without being blindsided from time to time. You know what I mean.

Most CEOs have exciting lives. They experience great moments like seeing their child score that goal, the vacation in Bali, nailing that target account, hiring the new A player, getting rid of debt from the balance sheet, buying that competitor, cashing out.

But while these CEOs are leading the climb up the mountain, major setbacks can also occur: a loved one dies; a spouse leaves; they are stressed out; they have a heart attack; their number one performer quits and joins their biggest, toughest competitor; the bank calls and pulls their line; their biggest customer goes bankrupt; they go bankrupt; so-called friends disappear.

The saying, "Life is what happens while you are making other plans" is so true.

I want to do everything I possibly can to help CEOs succeed, to help their families and their companies, to be a confidant and mentor to CEOs, and help them make their lives better in whatever way I can.

Why? Because it is a tough road to go alone and CEOs are often in a lonely place.

I wish I could do more.

Here is what I do:

- Bring CEOs together in a CEO peer group to learn from each other: CEOs helping other CEOs succeed by checking each other's backswing

- Provide access to a brain trust that can provide insights and honest feedback on a CEO's biggest opportunities and challenges

- Meet one-to-one with CEOs to discuss "the most important thing we should be discussing today"

- Listen carefully and ask the right question at the right time

- Be there in their corner, unconditionally

- Help veteran business leaders experience the satisfaction and fulfillment that comes from helping other CEOs succeed

People say to me, "How do you have so much energy and passion after so many years in business?" Because of the people I am with on my journey. These are the CEOs you will meet and learn from in this book, just as I do every day.

I am looking forward to introducing you to CEOs who walk the walk when it comes to being made, not born. These are people who work hard at staying sharp and keeping ahead of their competition by learning to be better leaders. They are always curious, always looking for ways to get better at the craft of leadership.

Throughout this book you will see me make reference to the term "CEO" often. I do this for ease, efficiency, and simplification. I use this term interchangeably with other words or phrases for people who have bottom-line responsibility, including presidents, entrepreneurs, and managing partners.

THE MODEL: THE SEVEN IMPERATIVES OF GREAT CEOs

In this book you will read about the "Seven Imperatives of Great CEOs." An imperative is defined as "something that demands attention or action; an unavoidable obligation or requirement; a necessity." Is imperative too strong a word? No. Whether you are an entrepreneur, a CEO, or a senior executive on your way to the top seat, these Seven Imperatives will allow you to learn, grow, succeed, and become Great!

The Seven Imperatives of Great CEOs are:

- **Emotional Intelligence:** understand yourself and others
- **The Ability to Inspire:** generate and communicate a great vision
- **Building the A Team:** find and keep the right people
- **Accountability:** take responsibility and get things done

- **Great CEO Tools:** use the best information to make quality decisions

- **Perfect Balance:** identify and create your perfect work–life balance

- **The CEO Connection:** accept the support and knowledge of your peers

The diagram below provides an excellent illustration of the interconnectedness of the Imperatives and the role a CEO peer group (The CEO Connection) plays in holding them together.

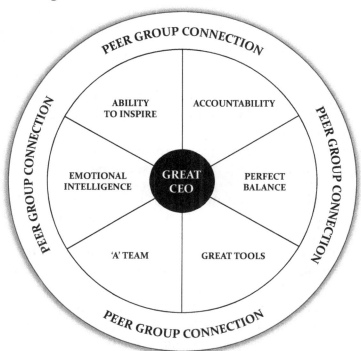

The CEO Connection is the Key Imperative. The connection to a trusted group of peers supports the efforts needed to tackle each of the other Imperatives.

Why?

Because CEO peer groups are all about CEOs helping other CEOs succeed. Peers bring many backgrounds, skills, and experiences to bear on a problem. Peer groups are a form of "informed empathy" that cannot be obtained in any other relationship. Peers are good at understanding what you're going through and where you're coming from because they've often been there themselves. They may be in a completely different business, but their experiences are usually comparable.

As a member of a CEO peer group you will hear the unfiltered, unmeasured truth. You will meet with this group of non-competing CEOs and your CEO Group Leader—your mentor, who is an instrumental part of the CEO Connection—every month to discuss the biggest challenges and opportunities in both your business and personal life.

Your CEO peer group members will offer honest feedback on your personal growth. They will provide valuable input on your vision and your business plans. They will give insight on work–life balance issues, on your numbers, on your goals. They will check your backswing and hold you accountable. They will share CEO tools: tools to help you build and keep an A team; tools to help you communicate; tools to help you lead. They will stand for your success. They will inspire you. They will listen, they will care, and they will help you be Great.

We will examine each Imperative individually, but keep in mind that they are not intended to be tackled sequentially, nor are they independent of each other. Be aware of how they are connected and how they work together.

The first Imperative detailed in the book is Emotional Intelligence. After joining a CEO peer group, it is the best starting point on your journey to Greatness. Only by understanding your own strengths and weaknesses—and the impact they have on both yourself and others—can you truly master the remaining Imperatives.

Begin with manageable steps and keep moving forward.

Remember: Greatness is not given; it is earned and learned!

Become Great and stay Great!

Chapter One

Emotional Intelligence:
The "Sine Qua Non" of Leadership

*"Emotional Intelligence opened a whole
new world of understanding for me. I instantly
felt the power of emotional self-awareness
and knew that the proper use of this tool in
a business environment would definitely give
Sherway a competitive advantage."*

~ Paul Rockett, founder and CEO of Sherway Group

L et's begin with the secret weapon of all Great CEOs: Emotional Intelligence (EI).

The impact that a leader can have on the outcomes that a business can create is enormous, both positively and negatively. One of my favorite expressions is "the speed of the leader determines the speed of the pack." For me, this captures the critical importance of the leader. It is the reason why CEOs must "keep the scalpel sharp."

Although a certain degree of analytical and technical skills is a minimum requirement for successful CEOs, studies indicate that emotional intelligence may be the key attribute that distinguishes outstanding performers from those who are merely adequate.

The two masters in this arena are Carolyn Robertson, MD, CEO and founder of The Centre for CEO Enrichment Inc., and psychologist and author Daniel Goleman, who wrote the best-selling book on emotional intelligence, *Primal Leadership: Learning to Lead with Emotional Intelligence.*

EI AND LEADERSHIP SUCCESS

Daniel Goleman is the person who brought the idea of emotional intelligence to the business world. It was Daniel who educated leaders on the subject by following up his 1995 book, *Emotional Intelligence: Why It Can Matter More Than IQ,"* with his classic 1998 *Harvard Business Review* article titled "What Makes a Leader?" Within the article Goleman states that *"to achieve improved business performance, leaders need to be emotionally engaged in their self-development."* He goes on to say that in examining the relationship between emotional intelligence and effective performance, his studies have shown that emotional intelligence is twice as important as both IQ and technical skill for jobs at all levels. Other competencies matter, he says, but mainly as "threshold capabilities," or entry-level requirements for particular positions.

"The ability to manage yourself—to have self-awareness and self-regulation—is the very basis of managing others."

~ Daniel Goleman, author of *Primal Leadership*

According to Goleman, emotional intelligence is the single biggest predictor of leadership success. While the importance of traditional intelligence, technical skill, and experience can't be underestimated, he has said that emotional intelligence is the *"sine qua non"*—the most essential aspect—of leadership. Without it, *"a person can have the best training in the world, an incisive, analytical mind, and an endless supply of smart ideas, but he still won't make a great leader."*

Here are the five components of emotional intelligence:

- **Self-Awareness:** the ability to recognize and

Primal Leadership: Realizing the Power of Emotional Intelligence by Daniel Goleman, Richard Boyatzis and Annie McKee, Copyright © 2002 Daniel Goleman. All rights reserved. Published by Harvard Business School Press

understand your moods, emotions, drives, and their impact on others

- **Self-Regulation:** the ability to control or redirect disruptive impulses and moods; the propensity to suspend judgment—to think before acting

- **Motivation:** a passion to work for reasons that go beyond money or status; a propensity to pursue goals with energy and persistence

- **Empathy:** the ability to understand the emotional makeup of other people; skill in treating people according to their emotional reactions

- **Social Skill:** proficiency in managing relationships and building networks; the ability to find common ground and build rapport

Of these, Great CEOs have three outstanding emotional intelligence qualities that help make them Great.

The first is that they are self-aware—they understand themselves, which means they are much better equipped to understand others.

The second most important quality is their high level of empathy or social awareness. They have the ability to understand where others are coming from, which comes from being self-aware and able to manage their emotions.

Their self-awareness and empathy help Great CEOs achieve the third most important quality: social skill— their ability to truly, genuinely connect with people—to relate ... to inspire.

POWERFUL LEADERS KNOW SELF

Early in my CEO confidant and mentor journey, as luck would have it, I met Carolyn Robertson. She became my own confidant and mentor.

You have heard the phrase "smartest person in the room"? Carolyn may just be the smartest person in the world when it comes to understanding the CEO brain. She works with CEOs and their teams to help them "kick it up a notch" by understanding themselves and those around them better. According to Carolyn, Emotional Intelligence is *"the ability to utilize information contained in emotions, yours and others."* She is absolutely the best at helping CEOs become more emotionally intelligent.

"Powerful leaders know self" is a phrase coined by Carolyn, and is the number one secret to "How They Are Made." In her training as a surgeon, she naturally utilized a scalpel. Now in her work with the brain, Carolyn determined that she has become the scalpel; cutting through thoughts and actions that can inhibit growth and success, and helping CEOs and executives keep their own mental scalpels sharp. Carolyn understands that whether real or metaphorical, only sharp scalpels are useful in getting the job done.

Every CEO I work with has an opportunity to work one-on-one with Carolyn to become a better leader through a greater understanding of this crucial imperative.

THE EQ-i SELF ASSESSMENT

One of the resources utilized by Carolyn Robertson is the

EQ-i. According to Carolyn, the results are a "doorway in" to a conversation with a CEO in an effort for them to begin to "know self."

EQ-i stands for Emotional Quotient Inventory and it was developed in the 1980s by psychologist Dr. Reuven Bar-On. EQ-i measures our ability to deal with the daily demands and pressures of life.

Dr. Bar-On believed that emotional intelligence was made up of a series of overlapping but distinctively different skills and attitudes that could be grouped under five general themes or "realms," and then further subdivided into 15 components or "scales."

In their book, *The EQ Edge*, Steven J. Stein, PhD, and Howard E. Book, MD, explain how Dr. Bar-On and MHS, a company founded by Steven, teamed up to take EQ-i to the next level. MHS began collecting data that fine-tuned Bar-On's initial findings and made them relevant to North American circumstances.

Since then, thousands of pilots, athletes, CEOs and executives have benefited from their EQ-i self-assessment. I have personally completed the EQ-i and have included a one-page summary of the report I received from MHS in the Appendix on page 184. Then, most importantly, I reviewed it in depth with Carolyn. I found it to be such a valuable experience that each of the CEOs I work with is given the opportunity to meet with Carolyn for two hours to review their EQ-i report and determine the number one thing they want to turn the volume up or down on in order

The EQ Edge: Emotional Intelligence and Your Success, 3rd Edition by Steven J. Stein and Howard E. Book, Copyright © 2011, 2006, 2000, Multi-Health Systems Inc. All rights reserved. Published by Jossey-Bass, A Wiley Imprint. www.josseybass.com

to become a more emotionally intelligent leader.

Here are Carolyn's bare-bones definitions of the five general themes and each of the 15 EQ skills assessed by the EQ-i:

Intrapersonal: self-awareness and self-expression

Emotional Self-Awareness: the ability to identify, understand, and express your emotions

Assertiveness: the ability to effectively and constructively express yourself

Independence: the ability to be self-reliant and free of emotional dependency on others

Self-Regard: the ability to respect and accept yourself

Self-Actualization: the ability to actualize your potential and willingness to continue to develop yourself

Interpersonal: social awareness and interpersonal relationships

Empathy: the ability to read and understand others

Social Responsibility: the ability to be a constructive member of a group, team, or organization

Interpersonal Relationships: the ability to establish and maintain mutually satisfying relationships of a give-and-take nature

Adaptability: change management

Problem Solving: the ability to effectively identify and solve problems in a methodical manner

Reality Testing: the ability to objectively validate your subjective experience with external reality

Flexibility: the ability to adjust to change

Stress Management: emotional management and regulation

Stress Tolerance: the ability to effectively and constructively manage emotions

Impulse Control: the ability to effectively and constructively control emotions

General Mood: self-motivation

Happiness: the ability to be content with life

Optimism: the ability to have a positive attitude

The EQ-i report is based on your responses to 125 statements such as, "It's difficult for me to begin new things," "My impulsiveness creates problems," and "I like everyone I meet." The magic to this emotional intelligence self-assessment is meeting with someone like Carolyn who is highly qualified to interpret the results and show how the 15 skills are interrelated and, most importantly, how they impact your performance as a CEO.

She helps CEOs select the one or two high-leverage areas to develop that will make them more successful leaders.

If the CEO is highly committed to getting better, then Carolyn continues to work with them and "holds their feet to the fire" to ensure they are effectively working toward positive change.

An analysis of top CEOs in *The EQ Edge*—based on profitability as the defining factor of success—interpreted the top three EQ skills of superstar CEOs as Self-Regard, Assertiveness, and Empathy. Complete an EQ-i self assessment and find out how you score on these three skills.

"Great leaders move us. Great leadership works through the emotions."

~ **Daniel Goleman,** *Primal Leadership*

STORIES OF SUCCESS

Right now, I would like you to meet three Great CEOs. They are CEOs with a high level of emotional intelligence to go with their high level of business acumen.

Paul Rockett is the founder and CEO of Sherway Group, an asset-based, full-service, customized logistics and supply chain solutions provider, which includes Rock City Cartage, Sherway Warehousing Inc., and Sherway Logistics Inc. It is one of the top-performing logistics companies in the world.

Paul is an outstanding leader and a lifelong learner:

Emotional Intelligence opened a whole new world of understanding for me. I instantly felt the power of self-awareness and knew that the proper use of this tool in a business environment would definitely give Sherway a competitive advantage.

Imagine your executive team clearly understanding each other's strengths and weaknesses and working together to help each other strengthen those areas that need improvement. Reminding one another of a tendency "to control" or "not be assertive enough," as examples.

Well at Sherway we have just such a team. We meet monthly for four hours to do nothing but work on self, which in reality develops the team. Egos are checked at the door. Our guide, Carolyn Robertson, helps clarify each of our EI tendencies, offers alternatives to negative behaviors, and provides cues to help us recognize these on our own. Discovering one's EI has fueled a path of change at Sherway. Our players have become more emotionally aware of self, and others, resulting in the team's success.

Chris Gower is the executive vice president of PCL Constructors Canada Inc., one of the top employers in North America. The company is 100 percent employee-owned and its annual construction volume is over $5 billion. It is the largest general contracting organization in Canada and the sixth largest in the United States.

Chris is at the top of his game in one of the most competitive businesses in the world. He is always learning and looking for ways to improve, and was recognized in

2009 as one of *Canada's Top 40 Under 40*™—an award presented to exceptional Canadians under the age of 40 who are outstanding leaders in their chosen field.

Here is how Chris feels about the importance of self-awareness for leaders:

For me the biggest learning experience has been recognizing how little I really knew about myself and being a leader. Now I've shed the arrogance, and allow myself to become more curious and introspective. I approach different situations with an open mind. I've realized that what got you here today won't necessarily get you to where you need to be tomorrow. I've also realized that humility is a friend, while arrogance can be your worst enemy.

Mike Reinders is a giant of a man. Doorways, airplanes, and beds were not designed for a guy the size of Mike. How big? Six eight. Big.

As the President of Maple Reinders Group Ltd., Mike has led his company through many levels of growth, and today the company is one of the pacesetters in the industry. From "green" projects such as water treatment plants, to designing, building, and operating leading-edge environmental facilities, Maple Reinders is at the forefront of technology in the construction industry and has been named one of *Canada's 50 Best Managed Companies*—a program recognizing excellence in Canadian-owned and -managed companies that have revenues over $10 million.

Mike is thirsty for knowledge. He is always learning and using that knowledge to get and keep an edge on the competition. He is self-aware, and it is a good thing that a guy this big is! Here are his thoughts:

I've come to realize that getting to know yourself is a very important part of growth, and a continual process until the day you die. You can't change who you are, but you can change some of your behaviors, how you react to things, and what you choose to do. I now enjoy helping others—my employees and family—get to know themselves better, improve their use of their gifts and abilities, and thereby become more successful.

ACHIEVING GREATER EI

The good news for all of us is that emotional intelligence can increase with age! And it can be improved at any stage of our lives if we have the motivation. How good is that?

"Great CEOs are self-aware, self-confident and self-regulated. These qualities make them benevolent leaders of people who make appropriate decisions for their companies because they are coming from a solid foundation. These three critical qualities all require higher order cortical functioning (Executive Functioning) so to achieve them is not a small feat."

~ Carolyn Robertson, MD

And everyone can get better. Myself included. Thanks to Carolyn Robertson, and a drive to become more emotionally intelligent, I am much more self-aware today than I was 10 years ago.

The key to getting better is to work hard at it. The key to working hard at it is to be motivated toward it. The key to being motivated toward it is to genuinely believe that emotional intelligence is a differentiator for all leaders.

On LeadingBlog, Michael McKinney, president of LeadershipNow, outlines the following 12 ways to achieve greater emotional awareness:

- Stop blaming others for your choices. It's you.

- Take a personality assessment to help you gain some perspective.

- Get feedback from as many significant people in your life as you can. This can be uncomfortable for both you and them, but it is the fastest method for gaining a better picture of yourself.

- Get a coach or mentor. They don't have to know more than you. They just have to see you in action and help you to be a better you. You're not as hard to figure out as you would like to think.

- Understand that your biggest irritations look a lot like you.

- Look beneath your behavior to reveal your assumptions and filters. They dictate how you see yourself and others and impact how you relate to them.

- Look at your roadblocks. Learn to separate facts from your interpretations of them.

- Analyze your interactions. A lot of negative interactions signal a selfish approach to life.

- Reflect daily on your behavior. Ask questions like: How do I handle difficulties? What do I think or do when I don't get my own way? How adaptive am I? Can I control my emotions? Do I tend to say what I'm thinking when I'm thinking it? Do I judge other people and create conflict? How do others relate to me?

- Organize your thoughts in a journal. It is one of the best ways to capture what is going on around you and inside you. Make a note of the casual remarks people make about you.

- Read books and go to seminars that help you rethink your assumptions and address your problem areas and blind spots.

- Be careful what you say. Words mean a lot. Your language reflects your thinking and attitudes.

In his award-winning *Harvard Business Review* article "What Makes a Leader?" Daniel Goleman closes his comments by saying, *"It is fortunate, then, that emotional intelligence can be learned. The process is not easy. It takes time and, most of all, commitment. But the benefits that come from having a well-developed emotional intelligence, both for the individual and for the organization, make it worth the effort."*

Be brave ... don't think about it ... just do it. The rewards are huge.

Your family will thank you for the improvements you make in your relationship with them. Your top management team and employees will thank you as well.

CEO Action Items to Get to Know Yourself

1. Read *Primal Leadership* by Daniel Goleman

2. Read *The EQ Edge* by Steven J. Stein, PhD, and Howard E. Book, MD

3. Complete an Emotional Intelligence Self-Assessment (EQ-i)

4. Find your "Carolyn Robertson" to help you establish your EI development priority and develop a plan for improvement

5. Solicit honest feedback on your progress

Chapter Two

═══════════════════════════════

The Ability to Inspire:
The Power of Vision and Passion

*"Employees today are apprehensive. They need
to know the destination and agree to it. They
need to buy in to where the CEO is taking them."*

~ Michael Burrows, CEO of Maple Lodge Farms

═══════════════════════════════

G reat CEOs inspire others to perform at the peak of their abilities. How do Great CEOs inspire?

The same as all great leaders do: with the power of vision and passion.

Think of the overwhelming response to Martin Luther King Jr. and his "I Have a Dream" speech, delivered in 1963 at the Lincoln Memorial in Washington, DC, in which he called for racial equality and an end to discrimination.

Think of John F. Kennedy's inspirational speech before a Joint Session of Congress in 1961, when he vowed to put Americans in space and on the moon before the decade ended.

Think of Shakespeare's Henry V, who before going into battle against France, rallied his troops with the famous *"we few, we happy few, we band of brothers"* Saint Crispin's Day speech that inspired and led his greatly outnumbered English forces to victory.

CREATING AN INSPIRING VISION

The ability to create and communicate an inspiring vision is one of the top qualities of all great leaders.

CEOs must determine a magnetic, compelling but realistic vision of how their organization will change and improve in the future and then effectively communicate, communicate, and communicate that vision.

Frank Geier is president of Gordon Food Service Canada, one of the leading food distribution companies in North America. He was also a recipient in 2003 of *Canada's Top 40 Under 40*™ award for his accomplishments in the areas of vision and leadership, innovation and achievement, impact, growth and development, and community involvement and contribution. It was Frank's management team that nominated him for this honor. Frank knows about inspiring people! According to Frank, *"CEOs must have the courage to develop a great vision for the future. They must be willing to take the necessary risks, both personally and professionally, to follow that vision regardless of what others may think or say, even if the journey becomes very difficult."*

"Do you want to spend the rest of your life selling sugared water, or do you want a chance to change the world?"

~ Steve Jobs when wooing John Scully, then CEO of Pepsi, to become CEO of Apple

---

So what is an inspiring vision? And how does a CEO create and communicate an inspiring vision?

An inspiring vision is not something created by a marketing team to be posted on a website.

An inspiring vision must be properly aligned, communicated, and executed across all levels of an organization from the top down. It must be delivered with genuine passion, based on clearly communicated values, and supported by trust.

Mike Reinders, the president of the Maple Reinders Group, is a master at creating and communicating an inspiring vision. Here are his thoughts:

It is really important to see and understand what is happening in the economy locally, nationally, and internationally in order to interpret and to foresee and predict. That is where the visionary part comes in ... where is our industry going, when, and how?

Then the next step is to settle where we should go and what that will look like, and to determine the best course of action to get there. This takes good judgment, passion, courage, and drive to move the organization to see, understand, and be inspired to go for the vision. And you need great people and ways to grow them in order to accomplish the vision.

Then comes communication—we need that to help the organization know and understand where we are going and how we will get there. Communicate that well and it will engage the organization in a big way. Communicate the strategy that you will use to achieve the vision.

All of the above have to be built on a platform of values like trust, candor, integrity, honesty, service, fairness, recognition, reward, and safety.

THE IMPORTANCE OF VALUES

Vision sets the strategic direction—the ideal "what" or "where." Values, on the other hand, speak to the "how" and the "why." Your core values regarding your business need to be defined prior to establishing a vision, as it is these values that will form the foundation of your management style and provide the rules used to carry out your purpose and realize your vision.

You need to believe in what you are doing and why.

Once defined, these values need to be made clearly visible to everyone, both within and outside the organization, in order for trust to be established.

Michael Burrows is CEO of Maple Lodge Farms, a company recognized in 2010 as one of *Canada's Best Managed Companies*. Michael is a prime example of a CEO who has a crystal clear vision for his company that is supported by strong values.

The Maple Lodge Farms vision is:

"We are our customer's favorite chicken supplier. Inspired by our family farming roots, we create genuine customer partnerships by being true to our word and bringing innovative thinking and a 'how might we' attitude to all we do."

Behind this vision, Michael and his team have identified clear values that they see as being essential to achieving their vision:

At Maple Lodge Farms we strive to:
- *Build open and honest relationships amongst each*

> *other and with our business partners*
> - *Clearly define goals and expectations and be accountable for results*
> - *Be passionate, have a bias for action and a "how might we" attitude*
> - *Share our experience and knowledge in order to become "the best we can be"*
> - *Be flexible, willing to learn and consider other viewpoints*
> - *Be approachable, attentive, fun-loving, inquisitive and creative*
> - *Always demonstrate integrity, trust, respect and fairness*
> - *Continue the values that got us here: humility, a respect for family and hard work*

Michael has buy-in from his team, and they are consistently hitting the ball out of the park. Understanding that the ability to effectively communicate the vision throughout all levels of the organization is key; Michael meets with his management team twice weekly to remind them of the company's vision and values, and discuss how they are doing as a team in the accomplishments needed to achieve that vision.

COMMUNICATING YOUR VISION

Some of the best tools I have ever seen to help create and communicate an inspiring vision come from Kraig Kramers. Kraig is author of *CEO Tools: The Nuts-n-Bolts of Business for Every Manager's Success*. Every page of his book has a practical profit-improving idea.

He is a great believer in "from the gut" communication. Keep it simple and get the message across. Kraig lives in Atlanta, Georgia and speaks to CEOs worldwide. He is a regular speaker at our CEO meetings. When I ask CEOs to name the speakers who have given them the most practical tools to improve their business, Kraig Kramers is always high on the list.

Kraig's CEO Tools for achieving and communicating an inspiring vision include:

1. Walking the Four Corners (W4C)

This is a great way to get employees to buy in on your vision. Great CEOs walk the four corners every day. "Un-isolate" yourself by getting out of your office every day and spending 20 minutes walking the four corners of your company. As Kraig says, *"Stop with one person, two at the most, and ask open-ended questions like: What do you see that I don't see? How can we make this better for our customers? How can we improve productivity in this area? How can we grow faster? Then,... stand back and listen."*

Time and time again, as a successful CEO, Kraig has found that your people will give you all the answers. The people in a company always know how to make it better, but as CEOs we can isolate ourselves and listen too selectively, mistakenly believing that we have all the answers. As

CEO Tools: The Nuts-n-Bolts of Business for Every Manager's Success by Kraig Kramers, Copyright © 2002 U.S. Corporate Partners, LLLP. All rights reserved. Published by Gandy Dancer Press

Kraig says, *"We have a special filter eliminating certain input and we're typically listening only to those advisors at the top. Very often we just don't even ask."*

2. Repeating the Message and Telling the Story

Articulate your vision and back it up with great stories. The best role model I can think of is Herb Kelleher, the co-founder and retired CEO of Southwest Airlines. He will always be remembered as being the inspirational leader of the most successful airline in the world. Herb is inspirational leadership on steroids.

You can imagine the pressure he faced as both competitors and regulators tried to put this upstart airline out of business. But he stayed true to his then revolutionary vision of low fares and high passenger satisfaction, and led the company to a 30-year string of profitable performance during a time when many other airlines were losing money and going bankrupt.

Herb was a master storyteller but also a masterful leader. He knew how to inspire people and how to make money.

Herb loved the employees of Southwest Airlines. He truly believed that *"people come first, and if you treat them right, they'll treat the customer right."*

Communication is key. Your team can't get you where you want to go if they don't know the destination or understand the directions. You must develop a strong and concise message and repeat it continuously. Whether in a monthly letter or a weekly email, it is crucial to clearly and consistently communicate with your employees. Share your business plans with everyone and meet with direct reports regularly. Don't worry about being repetitive. As Kraig Kramers says, *"repetition results in retention."*

"Don't underestimate the power of a vision. McDonald's founder, Ray Kroc, pictured his empire long before it existed, and he saw how to get there. He invented the company motto—'Quality, service, cleanliness and value'—and kept repeating it to employees for the rest of his life."

~ Kenneth Labich, journalist

GETTING ALIGNMENT

Great CEOs know that the effective execution of strategies to achieve their vision is critical. They know that effective execution depends on aligning the organization around these strategies. It is essential that everyone is on the same page and it starts with the top management team—the people reporting directly to the CEO. Everyone has to be pulling on the oars at the same time.

Verne Harnish has developed an excellent model for top-level alignment. His One-Page Strategic Plan is outlined in his book *Mastering the Rockefeller Habits* and, as Verne

Mastering the Rockefeller Habits: What You Must Do to Increase the Value of Your Fast-Growth Firm by Verne Harnish, Copyright © 2002 Verne Harnish. All rights reserved. Published by Gazelles Inc.

explains, *"It is a simple yet powerful tool that helps you edit your vision and strategy down to a single, action-oriented page."*

Verne's One-Page Strategic Plan is a working document based on the assumption that no organization or individual can focus on or accomplish more than five or six priorities in a given time period. It forces you to select your top priorities for each of the various vision pieces (values, purpose, targets, goals, actions, schedules, and accountabilities) and outline them in as clear, concise, and simple a manner as possible.

As Verne explains on the headline of every One-Page Strategic Plan he distributes: *"You must remember that this process is 1 percent vision and 99 percent alignment. The lion's share of your effort must not go into meeting, talking, and wordsmithing, but toward getting your people aligned to do what needs to be done."*

Verne's One-Page Strategic Plan is straightforward and thorough. It is intended to achieve alignment at a top management level. Once it is complete, you need to communicate its basic messages across your entire organization.

Kraig Kramers has developed a great tool that picks up the four major components from any strategic plan and pulls them into a one-page letter to be shared with all employees. This "One Page Business Plan" is one of the best tools I have ever experienced to get everyone across an organization on the same page.

As Kraig Kramers says in his book *CEO Tools*, *"There isn't a simpler, more effective tool than the one page business plan for getting employees focused on a big audacious fun goal or any other major company or departmental goal, and then for communicating how each of them can contribute to reaching it."*

Kramers' One Page Business Plan highlights four key components from a strategic plan:

1. Your unique business proposition: "why you?"
2. Your purpose: your customers and how you serve them
3. Your overall goal
4. Your strategy: where the company needs to go and how everyone will get it there

It is an excellent communication document to achieve alignment.

Verne Harnish's One-Page Strategic Plan should be created first, before preparing Kraig Kramers' One Page Business Plan, as Kramers' assumes that you already have a more detailed, strategic plan in place. Although similar, I recommend that everyone invest the time to prepare both documents. Together, they will provide a tremendous "one-two punch" that will help you visualize and articulate your vision and get alignment on your goals across your entire organization.

Another powerful alignment tool is having face-to-face, one-to-one meetings every month with each of your direct reports. These should be two hours, with no interruptions.

Great CEOs do this automatically. It is the highest form of communication between the CEO and the most important people in the company: their team of direct reports.

These monthly two-hour meetings with direct reports are the ultimate fierce conversations. Nowhere to hide. No way to not answer the questions. No way to make excuses for targets not met.

At the top of the agenda for this meeting should always be the question: What is the most important thing we should be discussing today? Or put another way: What is the best use of our time together?

Other regular agenda items should include reviewing Key Performance Indicators, discussing major strategic initiatives, and evaluating both team performance and self-improvement goals.

Many CEOs are so busy that they don't carve out the time to have these meetings. These are absolutely the most important meetings for a CEO.

Two hours, every month, uninterrupted time, and never in a restaurant or on a plane or in a car. This is golden time, and the time you spend in these meetings will buy you time and leverage it 100 times. I guarantee it.

John Piercy has led several highly successful companies including Mountain Cable, Atria Networks, and Shaw Communications. He agrees that the number one success factor for Great CEOs is communicating an inspiring strategic vision:

CEOs should have a clear understanding of where the company should be in three years and understand the various "alternative paths" to get there. This vision is required to properly weigh the more tactical decisions.

The CEO needs to be able to properly communicate both the long-term vision and short-term expectations of the company. This is more than an email–the CEO needs to ensure that there is strong alignment within the organization to the goals; and that obstacles and barriers to success are understood and can be overcome.

"For the first time, I feel like I can actually steer this ship. Sometimes you don't think about influencing outcome you just think about going for it. If you step back though, and build a vision, set goals, and then monitor your success, it's really rewarding. I feel like I have control over the destiny of this company."

~Shelley Wishart, CEO/Owner of Orchard International Inc.

THE POWER OF PASSION

To inspire others, Great CEOs must start by inspiring themselves.

Ask yourself where you are on the passion meter on a scale

of 1 to 10. Meaning, how strongly do you feel about your vision for the company? How do you feel when you wake up in the morning and know you are heading into work? If it isn't an eight or up you cannot—will not—inspire your team.

Allow yourself to be inspired by others. It is absolutely critical that your passion stay high. Great CEOs move people to achieve outstanding results through the power of communicating their vision with a genuine passion toward its achievement. If you ever feel your passion waning, check in with yourself and determine what is going on.

CEO Action Items to Create and Communicate an Inspiring Vision

1. Write an inspiring vision for your company

2. Get alignment on your vision across your organization:
    a. Read *Mastering the Rockefeller Habits* by Verne Harnish and create a One-Page Strategic Plan
    b. Read *CEO Tools* by Kraig Kramers and create a One Page Business Plan
    c. Conduct monthly one-to-one meetings with each of your direct reports

3. Communicate your vision across your organization:
    a. Walk the Four Corners
    b. Repeat the message and tell the story

Chapter Three

Building the A Team:
The Ultimate Competitive Advantage

"I will consider I have been a successful CEO if the company does better the more I step back, because I put the right people in place, doing the right stuff. I've got management in here that will take this company to a higher level than I have."

~ Dale Armstrong, CEO, Armstrong International Movers

Great CEOs learn how to find the A players, keep them, and inspire them. Nobody is born with this ability. It takes years of learning.

It takes a CEO who recognizes how critical the team around them is to their success. When I see CEOs floundering, drowning, stretching the goodwill of relationships all around them; I see CEOs who, for a long list of possible reasons, have not figured this out.

"Not finance. Not Strategy. Not technology ...
It is teamwork that remains the ultimate
competitive advantage, both because
it is so powerful and so rare."

~Patrick Lencioni, *The Five Dysfunctions of a Team*

So how do Great CEOs hire, nurture, and keep the A players?

First, figure out what they look like. By that I mean "what traits are you looking for?"

THE A PLAYERS

This is what Bradford D. Smart, author of the outstanding book *Topgrading: How Leading Companies Win by*

Hiring, Coaching and Keeping the Best People, says the best look like:

The Top Five Competencies of A Players are:

- **Resourcefulness:** the ability to get things done
- **Self-Awareness:** the ability to recognize and understand their own moods, emotions, drives, and the impact they have on others
- **Selecting A Players:** the ability to create a team of top guns and not be afraid to hire people who may be stronger performers than themselves
- **Redeploying B/C Players:** the ability to make the tough decision that B/C players just may be A players in the wrong positions
- **Coaching:** the ability to effectively develop direct reports and build winners

Of these, he sees the number one quality of A players as resourcefulness. They are strong in their driving passion to figure things out. Resourcefulness is a mega competency, as it is the ability to get things done, to get results, and put the numbers on the board.

One of the biggest reasons CEOs fail to build a team of A players is a false belief in their ability to "develop" a direct report who is not performing. They give the non-performer just too much time to turn their act around. It rarely happens.

Every CEO knows the number one Jack Welch rule: "hire slow ... fire fast." Unfortunately, many CEOs do just the

Topgrading, 3rd Edition: The Proven Hiring and Promoting Method That Turbocharges Company Performance by Bradford D. Smart, Ph.D. Copyright © 1999, 2005 Penguin Group (USA) Inc., Copyright © 2012 Bradford D. Smart. All rights reserved. Published by the Penguin Group

opposite and they pay for it in their company's performance, their performance, and ultimately, their job.

Another big reason CEOs fail to build an A team is their fear of conflict; fear of confrontation.

In Patrick Lencioni's book *The Five Temptations of a CEO*, he brilliantly outlines the top five things that can negatively impact a CEO's performance. These five temptations are:

- Choosing status over results
- Choosing popularity over accountability
- Choosing certainty over clarity
- Choosing harmony over productive conflict
- Choosing invulnerability over trust

Each of these temptations can be fatal for a CEO.

In true Patrick Lencioni terminology, some CEOs prefer being popular over being accountable and deciding that "Joe must go." Deciding to keep Joe has cost more CEOs their job than any other reason. They employ the "head in the sand" strategy and hope Joe will improve; hope Joe will come in and quit; hope Joe will go work with a competitor and mess them up. And yet ... Joe keeps showing up!

Everyone in the company knows "Joe must go." But the tough decision is never made.

The CEO gets fired and Joe gets his gold watch.

How depressing is that?

The Five Temptations of a CEO: A Leadership Fable by Patrick Lencioni, Copyright © 1998 Patrick Lencioni. All rights reserved. Published by Jossey-Bass, A Wiley Imprint. www.josseybass.com

According to Bradford Smart, author of *Topgrading*, the Joes of the world usually display one or more of the following 12 traits:

- **Lack of Resourcefulness**
  "too passive"
  "doesn't create opportunities"
  "always trying to delegate upward"

- **Not Selecting A Players and Redeploying B/C Players**
  "mis-hires too many"
  "has team of B and C players"
  "afraid to hire someone better than he is"
  "just won't upgrade"

- **No Passion**
  "not highly motivated"
  "lacks drive"
  "goes through the motions"

- **Lack of Integrity**
  "lies"
  "can't be trusted to keep promises"
  "breaks confidences"
  "gossips"
  "pushes legal boundaries too far"

- **Ambition**
  "too ambitious"
  "always trying to get the promotion rather than serve the company"

- **No Political Savvy**
  "a dirty politician"

"backstabber"

- **Not Adaptable**
    "over his head"
    "can't adjust to our reorganization"
    "job is too complex for him"

- **Not a Team Builder**
    "can't empower anyone"
    "control freak"
    "old-fashioned autocrat"

- **Not a Team Player**
    "builds silos"
    "thinks his department is the only one"
    "won't coordinate across departments, causing major production waste"

- **Poor Track Record**
    "missed his numbers again"
    "sandbagger"
    "more excuses than reasons"

- **Lack of Intelligence**
    "lacks the brainpower to adapt"
    "slow learner"
    "just doesn't get it"

- **Not Likeable**
    "arrogant"
    "condescending"
    "egotistical"
    "doesn't treat people with respect"
    "makes a mockery of our people values"
    "know-it-all"

"sarcastic"
"demeaning"
"acts superior"

"Do we have the right people on the bus? Do we have the right team that can take us to the next stage? No matter what business you are in, that is probably the biggest challenge that all CEOs face ... do we have the right people?"

~ Michael Burrows, CEO, Maple Lodge Farms Ltd.

THE COST OF NOT TOPGRADING

When I first read Bradford Smart's *Topgrading*, I was surprised to learn that every day that you keep the wrong person in the job costs your company almost 15 times their base salary.

Bradford should know. He worked with Jack Welch at GE for years creating A teams. He has a whole chapter in his book on the "financial and career costs of not topgrading." He clearly shows the cost of the wrong person in the job is $1.5 million per year for someone on your payroll with a base salary of $100,000. I knew the cost was high, but 15 times his or her annual base salary! Why so much? The opportunity cost of not having the person with the right stuff. As Bradford says, *"the single biggest estimated cost in mis-hiring is the wasted or missed business opportunity."*

And Bradford didn't even attempt to measure the costs of:

- your career stalling because you failed to topgrade and your team's performance was mediocre
- unhappiness of mis-hired people
- your wasted time and energy deploying B & C players
- your diminished fun and increased pressure because of your B & C player deficiencies

He goes on to say that it *"doesn't make any difference if a person is 'hired' from outside or inside the company. Mis-promoting internally is about as costly as mis-hiring an external candidate."*

Here is a recap of Bradford's *Cost of Mis-hire Study Results* based on 52 cases. The numbers shown are averages.

Number of years in job: 1.6
Base Compensation: $102,692

1. Cost in hiring:	$ 31,643
2. Compensation— all years:	$ 255,452
3. Cost of maintaining person in job:	$ 67,653
4. Severance:	$ 33,962
5. Cost of mistakes, failures, wasted and missed business opportunities:	$1,232,092
6. Cost of disruption:	$ 242,356
7. Sum of costs (#1– #6)	$1,863,158

Value of Contribution: $ 360,721

Net average cost of mis-hire: **$1,502,437**
(14.6 times base compensation)

Note that the single biggest estimated cost in mis-hiring is the cost of mistakes, failures, and wasted or missed business opportunities.

So, how many Joes are there on your team? In your company?

FINDING THE A PLAYERS

How do you find A players for the A team?

Let's learn from a CEO who knows. Jim Greenwood was CEO of his own company for many years. Finlay Greenwood was a successful food distributor that was acquired by one of North America's leading food distributors, Gordon Food Service Inc., which is headquartered in Grand Rapids, Michigan.

Jim went on to become responsible for all of Gordon Food Service's Canadian distribution business. He knows about finding A players and building an A team.

Here is one of his secrets for developing an A team:

> *One of the tools I like to use I call a Talent Audit. I create a color-coded organizational chart for each of the eight businesses showing individual employees' names in boxes. I color code each box on the org chart with one of five colors: Green is promotable. Blue is good or great in the job. Yellow is too new in the job to judge. Orange is I'm watching you because there is a potential problem. Red is you're on your way out of the business. I put the charts together for my CEO peer group and said, Okay, here is proof for*

me, I did this for myself but I am sharing it with you. Here are the sales-growth numbers and the performance of my eight businesses. The ones that have a lot of greens and blues have great sales growth. The ones that have a lot of yellow and oranges are the ones that are struggling. When I ever get in doubt that it is not all about the people, all I do is read this again.

Another secret weapon used by Jim and other Great CEOs to build A teams is Ed Ryan. Ed is one of the smartest guys I know when it comes to finding the A players.

Ed is the president and founder of Marketing Personnel Research Inc. (MPR), which is headquartered in Chicago. He works with CEOs all over the world helping them find the right people. At one time in Ed's early life he was a priest in the Chicago police department. He knows how to listen.

Now he listens to VP and CEO candidates to determine if they have the right stuff; the traits needed to outperform; to be a top performer.

Ed's Behavioral Benchmark Development Program is based on the competence theory: if you want the best, find out what the best do.

His program begins with an internal benchmark review. He asks you to identify the best performers in your company, and then these A players are tested and studied to determine what it is that makes them great at what they do.

Ed's benchmarking approach tells you what behaviors and traits a person in a given position within your organization must have to be successful. This benchmark is a powerful management tool.

Once they have identified the traits necessary for success, they then develop interview questions specific to that position within your particular corporate culture.

When the right benchmarks are in place, candidate profiles are measured against this detailed behavioral picture of the position, and you have a reliable, objective tool to help with critical hiring decisions.

As Ed says, *"Get the right people, in the right positions, in the right organization, and your whole organization will run like a well-oiled machine."*

We will talk more about Ed and his Behavioral Benchmark Development Program in Chapter 5.

A great tip from Ed is to keep a talent file. This is a file where you store the names and contact info of people who impress you. People whom you would like to have on your A team. Ed taught me to stay in touch with these talented people. Treat them like a customer you are nurturing. The people you want on your team will always be fully employed. You want to be there when they get a new boss, or the compensation model at their company changes to their detriment, or their company merges with another and the culture changes. Stay in touch with the A players you meet, and eventually they will be on your team.

BUILDING AN A TEAM

Building an A team begins with the hiring process, but

how do we ensure A players work effectively together to form an A team?

Patrick Lencioni's best-selling book, *The Five Dysfunctions of a Team*, has a great tool for your top management team to use to review its effectiveness. It will tell you and everyone on the team which one of these five dysfunctions is the most active within your organization:

- The absence of trust
- Fear of conflict
- Lack of commitment
- Avoidance of accountability
- Inattention to results

How much does it cost a company to have a dysfunctional top management team? One million per year? Ten million? Based on the "5 x earnings assumption," that will impact the market value of your firm by five times that amount. If we also factor in Bradford Smart's cost of not "topgrading," the cost balloons up to another 15 times that amount. That is a lot of money. Dysfunctional top management teams are worth fixing and Lencioni shows you how.

Patrick's Team Assessment will lead you to the dysfunctions you need to fix. The assessment is simple and involves honestly analyzing how each of 15 statements apply to your team on a scale of one to three, with one indicating "rarely," two indicating "sometimes," and three indicating "usually."

Sample statements include, "Team Members are passionate and unguarded in their discussion of issues," and "Team Members call out one another's deficiencies or unproductive behaviors." The lowest score is the number one dysfunction of your team.

As Patrick says, regardless of your scores, it is important to keep in mind that every team requires constant work, because without it, even the best teams deviate toward dysfunction.

It is worth repeating Patrick's excellent quote from the beginning of this chapter, *"Not finance. Not strategy. Not technology. It is teamwork that remains the ultimate competitive advantage, both because it is so powerful and so rare."*

The full version of the Team Assessment tool, including the scoring key, is available in Patrick's book *The Five Dysfunctions of a Team.*

Paul Rockett, the founder and CEO of Sherway Group, is one of the highest performing CEOs I have ever met. Paul understands the importance of building and nurturing a great team.

Here are the comments Paul made on teamwork to his employees in June 2010 as they began their journey to develop an outstanding top management team:

How often do you hear "They have the most talent but they were beaten by a better team?" Every sport that is played today has referenced this phrase so often it is now considered a sports cliché. Have you noticed we don't often hear about "Team" in the business sector?

Yet in boardrooms around the world, corporations are striving to assemble talent that is best suited to create the ultimate team ... to create a competitive advantage.

I have always talked about "Team" and firmly believe I have lived "Team." I have played, coached, trained, managed, and organized all my life. In the early days at Sherway, it was three people sitting down, discussing the best ways to tackle a job. Everyone gave an opinion and we would pick the one that [we] felt made the most sense and accomplished the task to everyone's satisfaction.

In hockey, I had three assistants. We would always consult each other in critical situations, often going against my original approach. Why have key people if you're not going to respect and incorporate their vision of what something should be?

Today, Sherway is starting a new journey. We have all the key elements of a strong team—with the guidance of Dr. Carolyn Robertson, the leadership of our President, Kevin Leggett, and my mentoring. Our goal is to create a working machine that has fierce conversation without ridicule and behind the scene sabotage.

A team is always made up of people with different characteristics. As you know we have begun to discover things about ourselves, with Carolyn's help. I want and need you to understand that everything we do with Carolyn and our team is for your betterment as a person. I firmly believe this will benefit you at home, at work, and in becoming a stronger team player than you had ever imagined.

So today we start by using the Patrick Lencioni model:

Trust: *Believe that your peers are well-intentioned and be comfortable in making yourself vulnerable to one another. This will result in focusing on the job at hand rather than fear or one-upmanship.*

Conflict: *Conflict becomes possible in the Team by building trust. When trust is present, open discussions happen. Productive conflict is necessary for growth and this will produce the best possible results in the shortest period of time.*

Commitment: *This just might be the easiest Team dysfunction to spot. We need to realize it cannot and should not always be "My Way." If your solution is not chosen as the best solution it is imperative that you back the decision of the Team.*

Accountability: *Be prepared to hold each other accountable and remember, if you have created trust and conquered the fear of conflict; your peers will know you are coming from a well-intentioned place when you are challenging them to improve.*

Results: *We must judge our success on common measurable goals. Along with profitability, we will be measuring the Team and each other by achieving these goals and driving profit.*

Using this model, I am confident we have what it takes to make a great Team. Carolyn will be guiding us on our journey to become the best Team possible. There will be bumps but hopefully not too many bruises along the way.

Carolyn is a professional who is strongly committed

to the well-being of everyone in this room. She believes firmly in treating the mind and the body for the best possible results. An undernourished body affects the mind. I have seen the results with my son Mark and myself—all positive! I like her approach and feel this is a pivotal decision for the future success for you as individuals and us as a Team, thus creating the Sherway Group Ultimate Competitive Advantage.

Like Paul, Michael Burrows realizes the important role a professional like Carolyn can play in helping a leader build an A team. Michael and his executive team have invested significantly in team development. Here is what Michael has to say about the Maple Lodge Farms team-building experience:

Carolyn Robertson facilitates an Executive Team becoming highly functional and "all it can be." She is the enzyme that gets you quickly there or to the fierce conversation.

She first delivers an insightful EQ/Myers-Briggs profile that establishes her credibility and gets your buy-in for the journey. Her focus is to build your self-understanding and your understanding of team members' behavior. She believes our past shapes who we are and how we act today.

She challenges us—and our team members—to be honest with each other, to learn about our true selves (how we behave and why). She asks the tough questions, goes deep to face the truth, and calls us out if it doesn't add up. The benefit is we become more trusting of each other.

Carolyn then adds in her intuitive piece, the "special sauce," an insight perhaps derived from pattern recognition. This becomes the permission to bring the real conflicts or issues to the table to talk about and resolve them. She creates an environment of "no fear."

The team journeys together, investing in each other. It is critical to meet on a regular basis to sustain the momentum and ensure progress via follow-up and accountability.

ONCE YOU HAVE THEM, YOU NEED TO KEEP THEM

Despite popular belief, money is not the best way to recognize superior performance. Keeping A players is all about meaningful communication and recognition. By meaningful, I mean it should not be generic or impersonal. Recognizing achievement with a gift card or game tickets without expressing the value you place on the individual's accomplishments is not meaningful. Communicating thanks in a note or in person without conveying that his or her contribution is *valued* is not meaningful. The communication and the recognition must be personal *and* authentic.

One of the best bosses I ever had gave me a great piece of advice: "Never miss an opportunity to be a good guy." He was tough, but fair—an excellent communicator. Most CEOs think they give too many compliments. They don't. Great CEOs turn up the volume on recognition.

Jack Daly is a highly successful entrepreneur and CEO. He founded and built a company that sold $350 million a month in mortgages, and earned $42-million profit in its first three years. He sold his company to a Wall Street firm and moved on.

Jack understands the importance of recognizing people and speaks from experience when he teaches CEOs worldwide how to create outstanding company cultures, "By Design Not Default." He is a must-see speaker, trainer, coach, and author, and speaks to the CEOs I work with every year.

He tells great stories, based on his many experiences, which highlight the importance of a CEO continually getting the A people in the key spots and then keeping them by being the cheerleader for the company's culture. Jack says *"to ensure your company's culture is right by design, it is critical to have the right systems and processes in place to bring the right culture alive."*

One of the most critical systems a CEO must have in place is an employee recognition system. By setting up a formal system you ensure that the right people will get recognized at the right time.

Jack is a big believer in Planned Spontaneous Recognition (PSR):

Planned: You need a process to recognize performance

Spontaneous: On a systematic basis, make the recognition unexpected

Recognition: Do lots of things that will let your people know they are valued and appreciated

This type of recognition can take the form of either

"things" or "events" and include anything from attending a sporting event with the boss to receiving a gift certificate.

Jack also recommends using consistent, anticipated forms of recognition, such as setting up a process by which employees in the company receive a handwritten note—sent to their home—from the CEO, on their birthday or their anniversary with the company. Other ideas include an "associate of the month" program, and the presentation of quarterly and yearly awards.

Christie Henderson is a great role model of a leader who knows how to nurture high performing teams.

Christie is the managing partner of Henderson and Partners LLP, one of the country's top firms of chartered accountants and professional advisors. She has developed an exceptional team that provides her clients with exceptional service. Christie believes that *"being successful as a leader is to have your team know that you have everyone's best interest at heart, and, that as CEO, you are always trying to do the right thing."*

Christie always takes the time to recognize and reward the many achievements of her team. She celebrates their success. These celebrations can include everything from bonuses to champagne. When members of her team have a birthday or anniversary, they receive a card and a poem written just for them. Big events in someone's life such as buying a new home, embarking on a dream vacation, or passing the CA exam are celebrated by the whole office. When the team completes a major engagement or project, a celebratory lunch is planned for them. Employees have even received trips with their family for some big victories or accomplishments.

Christie also believes in community involvement and feels that helping others gives her team a higher sense of pride and purpose. Employee satisfaction surveys are completed twice a year to ensure morale stays high and employee concerns are taken care of in a timely way.

David Dobbin is another master when it comes to recognizing his team of A players. David is the former president and CEO of Mobilicity. He was named one of *Canada's Top 40 Under 40* in 2006 and he builds companies ... fast! Here is one of his secrets:

> *For me, taking the time to make simple notes to remind myself to speak with someone for a job well done is just a matter of respect and being polite. I like it when I get recognized for good efforts and know others do as well. It can say so much to people when they see that you authentically want to say thank you. It is simple, easy, and timely, and does not have to be elaborate.*

In his book, *CEO Tools*, Kraig Kramers talks about the importance of rewards and recognition. Here are his top 10 tools for a CEO to become a better "recognizer" as well as his top 10 "Celebration Tools."

Top 10 Tools to be a Better Recognizer

1. Pat people on the back as they make headway on a job. Example: "It's great to see your progress on that project."

2. Talk positively about actual achievements of the company—daily. Example: "Our productivity sure is picking up lately."

3. Listen to people's problems. Example: "Would you share that with me?"

4. Give encouragement and compliment people whenever possible. Example: "You should try your idea about..."

5. Find ways of being helpful to those around you. Example: "I saw this article that may tie into what you're working on."

6. Tell people you believe they can do it, that you have faith in them. Example: "Looks like you'll set a new sales record this year. Keep up the great work!"

7. Generate hope; there's always light at the end of the tunnel. Example: "This storm will pass; they all do. We'll be better for the struggle."

8. Find ways to give good news to those around you. Example: "Did you hear the news about our profit growth?"

9. Get people to feel better, no matter how the interaction started. Example: "What can we do to make this work out better for everyone involved?"

10. Thank them for their effort, praise them for performance. Example: "Thanks for the hard work. And congratulations on winning that bid!"

Top 10 Recognition/Celebration Tools

1. Personal notes home. Send individual thank-you

and/or recognition notes to your people's homes to maximize the repetition of positive results.

2. Celebrate successes. Report against key goals and regularly celebrate the ones you achieve. Your people will respond with repeated superior performance.

3. Recognition buck$. To extend recognition, have employees recognize each other for positive actions. As Ken Blanchard said in *The One Minute Manager*, "Go out and catch someone doing something right." When you do, give them a Recognition Buck.

4. "Harley" hot button. Your key players won't buy it for themselves. Match something they really want or need—but can't or won't acquire for themselves, like a Harley-Davidson—to the achievement of a key goal.

5. W4C—Walk your four corners. Recognize and celebrate daily successes just by walking around and talking with people. Get the company's officers to shake hands and congratulate everyone on all three shifts. Get the CEO to go out and say "thank you" to someone every day.

6. Awards, awards, awards! Have monthly, quarterly, and annual awards. You can't over-do this unless you're the type that can't give awards. If so, get someone near you who can. Celebration is vital to an organization.

7. Recognizer's Top 10 tools. Take another look at the Top 10 Tools to be a better recognizer. If

there is one thing you take away from this chapter, it's go do your own version of employee recognition. Without question it's the biggest tool of all.

8. Two good celebration books. Read *1001 Ways to Reward Employees* and *1001 Ways to Recognize Employees* by Bob Nelson.

9. Silver dollars. As noted sales expert Chuck Reaves says, "Give 'em something hard and shiny!" People like hardware, so give them something that out-lasts us mortals. Give them your version of silver dollars or a similar symbol.

10. YCDBSOYB. Regularly inject fun into your business to keep you fresh and interesting. YCDBSOYB? You can't do business sitting on your butt.

The point is to look for creative ways to recognize and reward people, and do it often.

Ian Collins is the former president and COO of Atria Networks LP, a telecommunications and fibre optic service provider, which was acquired by Rogers Business Solutions. He is now the CEO/Owner of Claremont Holdings Inc. Ian makes an excellent point about Great CEOs being "real" in order to gain the commitment and loyalty of their team and keep their A players.

As leaders we don't always have the answers. The CEO should not be too proud to ask for help and engage people in transparent dialogue about the business. By being transparent in this regard the CEO develops trust in his people and that trust will lead them to offer constructive suggestions and to take more calculated risks that in turn will drive success. An engaged and committed workforce is the cornerstone of a successful company and nothing drives employee engagement more than the feeling they had a part to play in the strategy and execution.

Believe in the investment and in the growth of your people. Recognize that the staff—like the equipment used—requires regular maintenance to continue to perform at their peak. That training investment should be as fundamental as dollars spent maintaining your equipment. Providing those with expressed or observed potential, a career road map, and a plan to get to where they want to go, then providing opportunities to expand their span and domain of control, will lead to a high-performing, engaged workforce driving higher productivity, commitment, and lower turnover.

SUCCESSION PLANNING—WHO WILL LEAD WHEN YOU MOVE ON?

I often find myself sitting with CEOs or entrepreneurs who are thinking about retiring, or are coming to the end of their career and beginning to work their way through the succession process, thinking about the legacy they want to leave. I have spoken to hundreds of CEOs in this position.

This is a highly personal and often emotional time. Some executives handle it well, some less so. Often the difference is how well prepared they are. I encourage CEOs to consider the importance of choosing a successor, planning, mentoring, and setting that person up for success.

> *"Passing the baton is the final challenge of great leadership. If you do it poorly, or even drop the baton, you may do grave damage to your organization."*
>
> ~ **Marshall Goldsmith**, *Succession: Are You Ready?*

Succession planning is crucial if you want to ensure that all your hard work doesn't go to waste. CEOs therefore have to begin planning early, and do so carefully. Part of your legacy will be how well you did in creating an organization that continues to grow and succeed after you have stepped away. That is linked to how you prepared for your succession, and how well you prepared your successor and stood for his or her success.

A March 2010 survey done by OI Partners—a recruitment and executive coaching firm—among North American companies found that 71 percent had some form of succession plan in place, yet surprisingly and disappointing was just over half (54 percent) had curtailed their plans, or had let them lapse in the past year, saying they did not have enough "ready" people in their organizations to replace current executives and senior managers. Get ready—that is the point! Ladies and gentlemen, the talent crunch is on! If an immediate management change was needed, 40 percent said they would be forced to poach from the competition. Twenty-eight percent said their succession plan is to hire outside their company, and 14 percent indicated that they weren't sure that any of their current employees have sufficient talent to be developed into successors for top executive jobs.

YOU ARE THE ARCHITECT OF YOUR LEADERSHIP LEGACY

Succession at the top is critically important, in particular for entrepreneurs and family-owned businesses, but it extends far beyond that. The bigger concept is to get the right person in place for every job in the organization, including the successor at the top. That's the big win for an organization. If a firm desires to double in size over the next five to ten years, it will not be able to do so without having the talented resources required at all levels. Quality efforts made in support of mature, healthy, and candid succession conversations can help organizations and families long before the actual end-day arrives.

Clearly at the top rung, and for family-owned or entrepreneurial businesses, the development of future leaders and successors is key. Matching the organization's future needs with the resources of those available and the aspirations of the business is critical.

This is where a CEO peer group can help. Having an unbiased peer group to help CEOs think through their strategy and options can make a major difference. It definitely made a difference for Roger and Michael Grochmal of AtlasCare Heating and Air Conditioning:

Executive peer-to-peer learning is based on real people, real learning, real time, real issues, and real money. It is about understanding people—why they think the way they think—truly connecting with people, and recognizing outstanding performance. In my case, it is about family too. My greatest growth has been between my son and me. Michael works in the business with me. I am an engineer by training, and have always been strategic, analytical, process-minded ... find the best way and stick to it. My son is a sales guy, a relationship guy. We have different strengths and weaknesses. Over time there have been points of contention between us in the business. At some point, I will step down and plan to turn the reins over to Michael. In my heart I know he will do a great job ... just if he did things more my way! The challenge for both of us is that he is not me, and I am not him. With the help of some good coaches and our external executive groups—he in one group and I another—we are working our way through this for the better. Succession planning is critical in any business, but in particular family business. I intend to do everything possible to make sure it is a great success for him, our family, the employees and their families, our customers, and the business overall. This will be a part of my legacy.

Roger Grochmal, CEO, AtlasCare Heating and Air Conditioning

My Dad and I have been talking about succession and transition but he's often said well, you're not ready yet. I keep saying well, what am I not ready for? We have so many long-term employees—they are watching and waiting to see how much my Dad and I stick with this learning and manage our succession conversations and plans. It is our job to demonstrate to them that this isn't just a flash in the pan, this is a permanent corporate change, and we intend to do it right. I respect my father and what he has done. He is my best friend.

Michael Grochmal, VP Sales and Customer Care, AtlasCare Heating and Air Conditioning

In the time since Roger and Michael were interviewed for this book, Michael has successfully transitioned to the position of president of AtlasCare and the company continues to prosper.

It's important to recognize that one size doesn't fit all. The approach you choose will depend on the culture, processes, structure, and operations within your company. In some companies people will need to be exposed to a broad range of experiences fairly quickly; in others, longer exposure to certain departments will be required. Much also depends on the strengths, abilities, and experience of the people in key positions who are being groomed.

The good news is that by focusing on building and keeping an A team, natural successors will begin to materialize. From a Great team will emerge a Great successor!

CEO Action Items to Build an A Team

1. Read *Topgrading* by Bradford D. Smart

2. Create a Talent Audit for your organization

3. Define the benchmark behavior traits of top performers within your organization

4. Start a Talent File

5. Read Patrick Lencioni's *The Five Dysfunctions of a Team*

6. Complete Patrick Lencioni's Team Assessment and work on the biggest gap

7. Recognize at least one of your team players this week and every week for the rest of your career

8. Create a succession plan

Chapter Four

Accountability:
Taking Personal Responsibility and Getting Results

"I was in the middle of the worst year of my business career ever as the CEO of a furniture manufacturing company. We were losing money at a rate that was unsustainable. One of problems was that I had very little accountability in the business.

To increase my level of accountability and to get some fresh ideas on how to save the company, I joined a CEO peer group. These CEOs held up a mirror and forced me to see myself clearly, which was not always comfortable.

I put things on the table with them that I couldn't discuss with anyone else in the world. Their unfiltered feedback raised my level of awareness and encouraged me to take ownership of my destiny. They held my feet to the fire and reminded me of my accountability."

**~ George Sittlinger, President and CEO,
Maracle Press Ltd. and Oxygen Capital Corp**

George Sittlinger knows about getting honest feedback. Other CEOs holding him accountable dramatically improved his bottom line.

What do I mean by accountability? I mean: "The Buck Stops Here." It is about personal responsibility, execution, and getting things done. Accountability always begins with the person in the mirror. Great CEOs are accountable to themselves, their family, their business, their employees, and their community.

"An Accountability Fable"
Four people named Everybody, Somebody, Anybody, and Nobody, have an important job to be done ... and Everybody was asked to do it. Everybody was sure Somebody would do it. Anybody could have done it, but Nobody did it. Somebody got angry about that because it was Everybody's job. Everybody thought Anybody could do it, but Nobody realized that Everybody wouldn't do it. It ended that Everybody blamed Somebody when Nobody did what Anybody could have done ... and thus accountability was born."

~ Dan McCarthy, Director of Executive Development Programs, University of New Hampshire, Whitmore School of Business

---

Accountability often has a negative association attached to it. It can be interpreted as a tool for assigning blame or finger pointing. We need to think about accountability in a positive manner and create cultures of accountability based on personal responsibility for problem solving and goal setting.

Here is a great definition of accountability from the book *Journey to the Emerald City* by Roger Connors and Tom Smith: *"A personal choice to rise above one's circumstances and demonstrate the ownership necessary for achieving desired results ... See it! Own it! Solve it! Do it!"*

As CEO, you need to hold yourself accountable first, and in doing so learn how to help others achieve the same. By making yourself and your employees more accountable, you will make your organization more productive. There is real value in creating a culture of accountability. A culture of getting results ... of execution!

Taking a broader view of accountability can:
- Build stronger employees and teams
- Help revitalize business character
- Strengthen competitiveness
- Accelerate innovation
- Enhance quality of work, processes, and products
- Align organizations/functions

Boris Bratuhin is a CEO Group Leader. He is also the CEO (retired) of Toshiba Business Solutions. He knows firsthand about the importance of fostering a culture of accountability in companies.

There are certain basic things in business you have to do, and if you do them it will improve your business. And a lot of people just aren't doing them. I've had quite a few CEOs say to me that the biggest thing I've done to help them was to raise their levels of accountability and remind them to simply "do what you say you are going to do." Because over time, what can happen is, after putting in the years to build the business, the business starts doing well, they are making money, have a good lifestyle, and so they start to slack off mentally. They almost separate themselves and expect their employees to run the business. Many business owners and entrepreneurs fall into the trap of putting their business on automatic pilot. It is not intentional, many times it just happens. Then they start to see their business deteriorate. Or they see their employees coming in late, or even, not showing up. I say, "Well they look at you, if you're not accountable for the business, why should they be?" By getting these leaders focused again, resetting their accountability dials, things start to move forward in their organization and they find that they are enjoying it again, and learning and growing again.

A HIGHER AUTHORITY

Jamie Moody is president of Tree of Life Canada, one of the largest distributors of specialty and natural foods in Canada. As Jamie says, *"My CEO peers improve my chances of success. It is difficult to lead an organization by yourself without peers giving me candid honest feedback to build my level of accountability on the important stuff and hold me to it."*

Jamie has hit the nail on the head. This is the secret to being accountable. Have people around you who will tell you the truth. Check your backswing. Point out your blind spots. It all starts with trust.

"My CEO peer group provides me with an objective view of our business, and lets me know when I'm getting off track. It's a huge confidence piece."

~ Bill Kooy, President and CEO, Kooy Brothers

Everyone needs to be accountable to a higher authority. Who is the higher authority for the CEO? Who is your higher authority? Who is holding you accountable? Accountable on the stuff you must do, not just the stuff you want to do.

Other CEOs who want to see you succeed—leaders who stand for your success and want you to stand for theirs—can become that higher authority, if you let them. Great CEOs let them.

CEOs holding other CEOs accountable to do the right thing; to make the tough decision, not the popular decision.

When CEOs feel isolated with some of their decisions, a

CEO Group Leader is their outside accountability partner, checking their backswing, asking the right and often hard questions. They are a sounding board for them ... challenging when necessary and providing encouragement and helping them see their progress. They are not there to hold their hand, but to help them achieve their desired success.

Most CEOs appreciate, want, and need that candor. Having someone with credibility—another CEO—telling it like it is. That's a big part of how Great CEOs are made: by having the courage to hear the truth. It might be uncomfortable but hear it!

"Sometimes a [peer group] just gives you that kick in the pants to do something that you knew you had to do. They hold your feet to the fire ... no more excuses."

~ Helen Pike, VP of Marketing, Tree of Life Canada ULC

Shelley Wishart is the CEO and owner of Orchard International Inc., a highly successful company that specializes in developing innovative, creative gift and promotional items for bath, beauty, home décor, and gift industries.

Shelley founded the company in 1993 and it now has operations in Canada, China, and the United States.

Here is what Shelley has to say about accountability:

I'm responsible for the sales and the creative end of our business, but I never managed my sales department very closely. I had always worked under the assumption that they were working as hard as they could and I wasn't going to bother them. So I never set any particular goals for them. But after working with my coach and Group Leader, I now go out of my way to make sure that I go to the weekly sales meetings and ask the sales group about their prospects and results. As a result, the team is definitely better focused. They are prospecting more and our sales have increased significantly because of it. In the beginning I wasn't used to this kind of structure, but you can't argue with the results.

CREATING A CULTURE OF ACCOUNTABILITY

Communication and clarity are both key to accountability. It is crucial to clearly define and communicate goals and responsibilities.

Says Boris Bratuhin:

I'm surprised by the number of executives that don't share information with their employees. They develop business plans, but they don't share them. If you want your employees to buy in on what you're thinking, you've got to share it with them. How are they supposed to own the outcomes if they don't know what they are supposed to be?

I'm a firm believer that you need to build a certain culture to get everybody buying in. You should be able to walk into your warehouse or onto your manufacturing floor and ask any employee, "What is our purpose? What are we try-

ing to accomplish here?" And if you have the right culture, they should be able to give you a reasonable answer. If they say, well, my job is to put wheels on the car, and that is what I do, and that is the only reason I'm here, you have some work to do. I find it amazing how many employees have little or no idea what they're at work for, no idea what the company does. They only know the specific job they do. Connecting all those dots is very helpful and contributes to a culture-building process, raising levels of accountability across the organization.

"I've really enjoyed and benefited from the monthly coaching sessions and group meetings. These are all about accountability. It's a really great process, because you're expected to deliver on your promises. Your coach asks the tough questions because they want you to be more successful. Don't get me wrong: they don't tell you what to do; they just make suggestions and get you to think about your objectives in a different way."

~ Roger Grochmal, CEO of AtlasCare, Heating and Air Conditioning

---

Outstanding writer and speaker Patrick Lencioni has written several tremendous books on leadership including *The Five Temptations of a CEO* and *The Five Dysfunctions of a Team.* I have learned from all of Patrick's books and one of the major lessons is on the topic of accountability.

According to Patrick, one of the five temptations of a CEO is "Choosing popularity over accountability." By which he is referring to things like:

- being a close friend to your direct reports
- being bothered if they are unhappy with you
- hesitating to give negative feedback or watering down your feedback

Patrick also highlights that one of the five dysfunctions of a team is "Avoidance of accountability." This is manifested when the need to avoid interpersonal discomfort prevents the team members from holding one another accountable for their behaviors and performance.

Patrick Lencioni has great ideas around accountability that will make you a better CEO and everyone on your team more accountable. When he spoke to our CEO Group several years ago we learned about The Four Meetings as featured in his book *Death by Meeting*:

- The Daily Check-in (5 to 10 minutes)
- The Weekly Tactical (45 to 90 minutes)
- The Monthly Strategic (2 to 4 hours)
- The Quarterly Off-site Review (1 to 2 days)

Here is how each of The Four Meetings work:

The purpose of the 5- to 10-minute Daily Check-in is to share daily schedules and activities. It is intended as a brief, focused meeting. Patrick told us that the key to successful Daily Check-in meetings is to make sure they are stand up meetings—meaning literally—no sitting down. Make sure they are administrative and be consistent. In other words don't cancel the meeting even when some members of the team can't attend.

The major purpose of the 45- to 90-minute Weekly Tactical Meeting is to review the weekly activities including the metrics. This is also the place to resolve tactical obstacles and issues for the members of the team. The keys to success for this Weekly Tactical Meeting are to not set the agenda until after the initial reporting from everyone, to make tactical decisions only, and postpone any strategic decisions.

The 2- to 4-hour Monthly Strategic Meeting focuses on the critical issues affecting long-term success. This is where these issues are discussed, analyzed, brainstormed, and decided upon. In this meeting it is critical to not overcrowd the agenda. Limit the discussion to one or two topics. Two other important success factors for this meeting are first, make sure that everyone is prepared and the essential research has been completed and second, that the group avoids one of the five dysfunctions of a team, which is the fear of conflict. Great teams engage in constructive conflict because they are built on a foundation of trust.

The purpose of the 1- to 2-day Quarterly Off-site Review is to review the company's strategy, step back to evaluate what the competition is doing, discuss the big industry trends, review key people in the company, and discuss team development. Patrick reinforced the importance of having this meeting off-site with a focus on work and a limit to social activities. He also told us how important it is to not overstructure or overburden the schedule for this meeting.

Patrick's Four Meetings method is a powerful way to increase your accountability and the accountability of every member of your team and every member of their team. It works!

Add this to one of the best ways I have ever experienced for CEOs to be held accountable on the tough and, at times unpopular, decisions—a CEO peer group—and you WILL get results.

Here is what Jamie Moody, president of Tree of Life Canada, has to say about utilizing Patrick's Four Meetings and CEO peer groups to build accountability:

Every leader has heard the Jim Collin's lesson about having the right people on the bus and in the right seats. I think perhaps even more important is to have the senior team operating as one team, responsible first to each other, rather than the functional silos that they manage and most likely grew up in.

It was not always like this and we are still on the journey to improving our skills as a group. Our recent 360 feedback has helped identify things that each of us needs to improve individually and as a team. The good news is that everyone believes we can be better.

We started over six years ago working on how to cor-

rect some of our team dysfunctions. The group was a little different then and clearly we were not working as an aligned team. The functional imperatives still drove a lot of agendas. One of the early things we did to start was to improve me. I had the VPs and Directors (our National Staff) together at an off-site strategy session that began with a review of Lencioni's The Five Temptations of a CEO. They had all been given copies of the book and I asked them to think about and report on the temptations that I am guilty of. This had two positive impacts: first, I got some really great feedback on things I had to work on, and second, it set the stage for a more introspective view of what each of us may be guilty of as leaders. And it helped make it okay to admit that we all had areas for improvement.

One night, sometime after this, I was flying home from some meetings, and catching up on emails on the plane. There were a few issues going on in the business and a barrage of emails between our VPs really irked me. Clearly we were still protecting our functional turf and issues were not being resolved. The next day, I called the senior team together, expressed my disappointment over the lack of accountability and set a meeting for the following week. The purpose of that meeting was to see if the current team could build some trust. I asked each person to put together a list of their individual strengths and also their weaknesses, particularly around how they need support from others on the team. We started that meeting using the connectedness circle that members of my CEO peer group had taught me. Each person made a circle with everyone's name on it and put a number from 1 to 10 by each name—10 if you feel truly connected and comfortable with that person and 1 or anywhere in between being less connected. Having each one read out their connectedness by person got the session really going; especially when they described why they felt that way. In our group, it brought some emotion to the fore and made for a more honest review of each person's opportunities for improvement. The good news is that everyone cared deeply. The sad news was that not everyone could get on the same page and I ended up releasing a couple of the VPs from the team.

This redefined sense of "Team" is maintained and reinforced by our everyday practices now. Our daily stand-up "Check-ins" help us understand each other's priorities and issues for that day and particularly where one person needs help from another. These typically take 10 to 15 minutes and are done standing up to keep them short. Our Weekly Tactical Meeting focuses on our tactical goal. This goal is defined as our single most important priority to make the month, the quarter, or whatever timing window the goal needs to be accomplished within. The meeting rhythm is rounded out with quarterly meetings and an annual off-site meeting where we tackle more strategic issues and a mid-term (three to five year) planning horizon. We will also set our annual goals and objectives for the teams in one of these meetings.

Perhaps the final piece of our accountability process is our monthly one-to-one meetings—I have a monthly one-to-one meeting with each VP to discuss whatever they want to talk about. They set the agenda for the meeting and I try to be the best listener I can be, asking questions where appropriate, but making sure they have a protected time period each month to review issues and opportunities.

We are so much better as a team now that I cannot imagine having it any other way. And our financial results have consistently improved over this journey.

After all, life is not about assigning blame or making excuses, it is about taking responsibility. I think we have made considerable progress on this.

As the CEO you must get results. You owe it to everyone. And to get results you must be held accountable and you must hold your team accountable as well.

CEO Action Items to Create a Culture of Accountability

1. Read Patrick Lencioni's *The Five Temptations of a CEO*

2. Read Patrick Lencioni's *Death by Meeting*

3. Implement Patrick Lencioni's Four Meetings

4. Define and communicate goals and responsibilities across your organization

5. Become a member of a CEO peer group and receive honest, unbiased feedback

Chapter Five

Great CEO Tools:
What You Need to Succeed

"When I first joined my CEO Group my head was spinning like a top. Very quickly I learned about the key indicator dashboard. It was amazing what I learned and how well it worked.

Previously, I had been operating the business with a blindfold on ... feeling my way through it. Getting the right information so we could make quality decisions in a timely manner was a godsend for our business and has allowed us to grow dramatically over the past 10 years. I never would have learned about them without the help of my CEO Group.

Now I know where we stand. I have been able to reduce my anxiety level dramatically. It has turned my world around completely. I feel so much better about the business and have a more thorough understanding of the issues swirling around me."

~ Bill Kooy, President and CEO, Kooy Brothers

G reat CEO tools are an important imperative for Great CEOs.

As a student of business, I am always on the lookout for great tools that will help CEOs succeed, and I have had the privilege of working with and learning from outstanding people.

From their lessons, I have boiled everything down to my all-time top tools for CEOs. If you implement the tools in this book, I guarantee you will significantly improve your life, the life of your family, and the performance of your company.

We have discussed several of these tools in previous chapters, including:

- Patrick Lencioni's **Four Meetings** and **Team Assessment**
- Kraig Kramers' **Walking the Four Corners, One Page Business Plan, Top 10 Tools to be a Better Recognizer** and **Top 10 Recognition/ Celebration Tools**
- Verne Harnish's **One-Page Strategic Plan**
- The **EQ-i Self Assessment** developed by Steven J. Stein, PhD, and Howard E. Book, MD

In this chapter we will look at seven additional Great Tools.

Two of these tools focus on feedback for the CEO. They are the CEO Report Card and the Leadership 360.

The Ed Ryan Magic will help you find the A players and

Gary Markle's Performance Management System is the catalyst for CEOs to become better coaches for their team.

Kraig Kramers' Quarterly Priorities Management (QPM) also makes it on the list as it is an outstanding way to ensure your team is fully aligned and that all are held accountable to their goals.

Every CEO will also benefit from Susan Scott's Confrontational Model for dealing with an issue before it is too late.

But first, let's hear from some successful CEOs on the importance of knowing the numbers and the impact of two great tools—the Hartman KPI template and the Trailing 12-Month (T12M) Charts, developed by Kraig Kramers.

TOOL—THE NUMBERS: THE HARTMAN KPI TEMPLATE AND KRAIG KRAMERS' T12M CHARTS

Grant Heggie is the president and CEO of Melmart Distributors Inc. He feels that one of the critical success factors for any CEO is to *"get to the right numbers, know the right numbers and track them. It is critical to realize the impact of certain numbers on your business. Too many leaders don't know the numbers that drive their business and lead to profit. When you know the magical number set that works in your industry and your business, you can set your rudder on those numbers and with occasional trimming keep the organization profitable over the long haul."*

As Rick McClelland, the former CEO, chairman of the board, and director of Dynamex Inc. says, *"Establishing metrics and ongoing related measurement can enable people to accomplish important things for a business—and that is VERY motivating to most people because it creates a sense of purpose, a sense of belonging, a sense of accomplishment and confidence as they approach and hopefully surpass targets and goals. Motivated, focused people on your team will do a better job of getting customers, keeping customers, and helping you operate a profitable business. You can think of that as "enhanced growth capacity."*

Great CEOs know their numbers—the key numbers for their business. One of the top reasons CEOs fail is an aversion to the numbers. They leave it up to their CFO or Controller. Don't. Great CEOs have a deep understanding of the numbers.

The Hartman KPI Template

There are many tools available to track key performance numbers and many versions of key performance indicator (KPI) "dashboards" available, but the best financial tool I have seen is the one-page KPI template dashboard developed by Steve Hartman. It has all the key numbers on one page. Steve Hartman is the CEO and founder of Industrial Thermo Polymers Ltd. Several years ago, he took a financial report we were using and made it much better. Thanks, Steve.

See it updated daily ... weekly ... no less often than monthly.

Its value is in its simplicity.

It includes the key numbers from the income statement

and balance sheet for the current month and year to date, compared to the budget and previous year.

On page 96 is an example of the Hartman KPI template.

Add to this your T12M Charts for revenue, gross margin, expenses, and EBITDA. A Trailing 12-Month Chart identifies future problems and opportunities, giving CEOs the time to take action before the company "goes off the rails."

Kraig Kramers' T12M Charts

Here is how it works. Each dot on a T12M Chart represents a KPI for the previous 12 months ending in that month. It is a rolling annual total of the KPI—such as sales, gross profit, or EBITA—entered monthly, that eliminates the seasonality effect in looking at your results. As Kraig Kramers says, *"It is the only chart in the world that tells the truth, eliminates seasonality and points you to correct action."*

On page 97 are examples of Kraig Kramers' T12M Charts.

Cliff Sarjeant is the owner of NCI Canada Inc., a successful company that sells plumbing supplies such as piping and valves to a network of distributors and major retailers nationally. Cliff is a CEO with an excellent understanding of the numbers. He looks at the critical numbers every day.

Every time I meet with Cliff he has his KPIs and T12Ms front and center on his desk. As the leader of his company, he values the metrics of business and knows how important it is to be on top of them.

Sample Hartman KPI Template (for Company XYZ)
For Period beginning Dec 1/07

	JAN 2008				JAN 2007			
	ACTUAL	% TO SALES	BUDGET	% OF BUDGET	ACTUAL	% TO SALES	BUDGET	% OF BUDGET
NET SALES	$1,791,663		$1,767,500	101.4%	$1,619,958		$1,300,000	124.6%
GROSS MARGIN	$404,235	22.6%	$298,511	135.4%	$589,271	36.4%	$214,437	274.8%
TOTAL EXPENSES	$1,500,653	83.8%	$1,621,157	92.6%	$1,280,754	79.1%	$1,176,937	108.8%
DEPRECIATION	$25,226		$27,088		$28,701		$23,775	
EBITDA	$330,198	18.4%	$193,543	170.6%	$382,902	23.6%	$158,316	241.9%
NET PRE TAX	$291,010	16.2%	$146,343	198.9%	$339,204	20.9%	$123,063	275.6%

YR TO YR ACTUAL	
+/-	%
$171,705	10.6%
($185,036)	-31.4%
$219,899	17.2%
($52,704)	-13.8%
($48,194)	

From "Chart Data"
Input from Forcast/summaries

	FY 2008				FY 2007			
	YTD	% TO SALES	BUDGET	% OF BUDGET	YTD	% TO SALES	BUDGET	% OF BUDGET
NET SALES	$2,457,228		$2,912,500	84.4%	$2,499,089			94.3%
GROSS MARGIN	$331,752	13.5%	$482,089	68.8%	$379,677	15.2%	$435,126	87.3%
TOTAL EXPENSES	$2,405,963	97.9%	$2,709,755	88.8%	$2,395,001	95.8%	$2,214,874	108.1%
DEPRECIATION	$50,873		$54,588		$57,903		$53,769	
EBITDA	$129,813	5.3%	$289,181	44.9%	$191,498	7.7%	$515,925	37.1%
NET PRE TAX	$51,265	2.1%	$202,745		$104,088	4.2%	$435,126	

YR TO YR	
+/-	%
$41,861	-1.7%
($47,925)	-12.6%
$10,962	0.5%
($61,685)	-32.2%
($52,823)	

From "Chart Data"
Input from Forcast/summaries

EBITDA NUMBERS DO NOT REFLECT SHAREHOLDER DRAWS

	FY 2008	FY 2007	CHANGE
OPERATING LINE	$2,620,000	$2,410,000	$210,000
LONG TERM	$785,548	$802,073	($16,525)
RECEIVABLES	$2,234,034	$2,297,843	($63,809)
DAYS OF RECEIVE			
PAYABLES	$571,520	$614,372	($42,852)
CURRENT RATIO	1.56	1.46	0.10
DEBT TO EQUITY	0.977	1.13	

Sample T12M Charts (for Company XYZ)

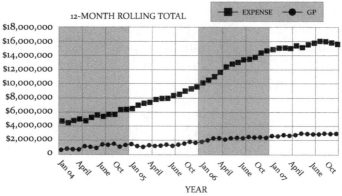

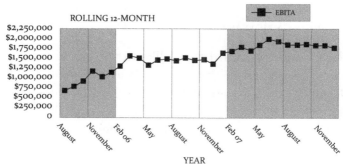

Kraig Kramers teaches CEOs worldwide the importance of KPIs and T12Ms. If he could only use one tracking tool, it would be the T12M chart because, as Kraig says, *"nothing gives you a truer picture of what is going on in your company."*

TOOL—CEO REPORT CARD

A great way for a CEO to get clarity on the number one thing they need to get better at, is to grade themselves on a CEO Report Card and see if they give themselves a passing grade on the important subjects. This first step is a self-assessment. Where are the gaps, and what are the priorities, in the CEO's opinion?

This exercise also helps newly appointed CEOs understand their job description. Many new CEOs simply don't know. A CEO Report Card definitely helps new CEOs understand their new world.

The next step is to get anonymous feedback from their direct reports by having each one fill out a Report Card and give the CEO a grade on every subject. Then, the CEO's Group Leader reviews the Report Cards from each direct report, and matches up the results with the CEO's self-assessment. This provides great clarity for the CEO's development priorities.

The CEO Report Card that I like to use evolved from an article published in the *Atlanta Journal-Constitution* on December 16, 2001, entitled "Report Card on Coke's CEO: Does Doug Daft make the grade?" In this editorial, a group of 11 industry experts evaluated Daft's performance in each of five areas: leadership, management, financial performance, marketing, and innovation. I took their questions, made a few changes, and came up with the following:

Leadership

Has the CEO set a compelling strategic vision for the company?

Has he or she communicated the vision to the management team and all employees?

Do the financial results show the company is aligned with the vision?

Is the CEO a good listener?

Empathetic?

Management

Is there an A team in place to achieve the vision and the strategic plan?

Is there an effective performance management system in place?

Are people being held accountable?

Is there a succession plan in place?

Financial Performance

Is the company putting the numbers on the board?

Is the budget being met or exceeded?

Is the company growing at the planned level

for both revenue and profit?

Does the CEO have a solid understanding of both the income statement and balance sheet?

Marketing

Is there a top-notch sales and marketing team in place?

Are they hitting their numbers?

Is there the right amount of money being spent on training and developing the sales and marketing team?

Are they beating the competition?

Is an effective recognition-and-rewards system in place?

Operations

Has the CEO put in place the right processes and procedures to ensure ongoing improvements to the operational activities of the company?

Are the right incentives in place to ensure continuous improvements in delivering what is important to our customers, e.g., on time, every time, as ordered?

Is there an effective performance measurement system in place?

Innovation

Does the CEO value innovation?

Is the CEO a "change agent"?

Have there been significant innovations that improved the company's sales and profitability under the CEO's leadership?

Using a scale of 1 to 10 with an "A" being a 10 and an "F" being a 1, what would you grade yourself on each question? How would others grade you?"

This CEO Report Card will give you valuable feedback on the things that you need to focus on to become a better CEO.

TOOL—THE LEADERSHIP 360

Marshall Goldsmith is the father of Leadership 360 feedback, which involves seeking confidential feedback from direct reports, peers, and bosses. He is also the author of the must-read book for every CEO and executive entitled, *What Got You Here Won't Get You There: How Successful People Become Even More Successful.*

Great CEOs encourage feedback constantly. This is how they keep on top of their game. They get feedback on their leadership and then act on any "gaps" between their perception and the perception of those that they lead.

Marshall's approach is brilliant. Marshall has a PhD from UCLA and over 30 years experience measuring and analyzing behavior in companies. He works one-on-one with very successful people who want to be even more successful. He helps them see that what got them to their current level of success probably won't get them to the next level.

Marshall enrolls his leaders in what he calls "a brutal regimen."

The first step is to get 360 feedback from as many people as possible. The term 360 refers to the "circle" of colleagues around the leader. These people are asked for a detailed assessment of the leader's strengths and weaknesses.

Then Marshall meets with the "victims" and gives them the unfiltered truth of how others see them.

He then shows them how to close the gaps on the biggest, most serious issues standing in the way of the leaders becoming even more successful.

Marshall teaches leaders to apologize for the gap, advertise their efforts to get better, and then follow up every month to determine if they are making progress.

He also teaches them to "listen without prejudice" to the feedback without interrupting or arguing and just say *"Thank you."*

Most importantly, Marshall teaches leaders "the miracle of feedforward." This is his special sauce for *"eliciting advice from people on what they can do to get better in the future."*

"Powerful Leaders Know Self"

~ Carolyn Robertson, MD

CEOs I work with have the opportunity to have their team give them feedback on their leadership performance by participating in a Leadership Practices Inventory (LPI).

This is a highly acclaimed tool, developed by Jim Kouzes and Barry Posner, for assessing leadership behavior. Jim is the Dean's Executive Professor of Leadership, Leavey School of Business, at Santa Clara University, and Barry is the Dean of Leavey School of Business and Professor of Leadership at Santa Clara University in Silicon Valley, California.

This Leadership 360 is based on the best-selling book by Kouzes and Posner, *The Leadership Challenge*. The book speaks to their 25 years of research on "what people did when they were at their 'personal best' in leading others."

Their LPI is one of the most widely used leadership assessment tools in the world. More than 350 doctoral dissertations and academic research projects have been based on their model.

The LPI is a 360-degree questionnaire for assessing leadership behavior. It is valuable tool to help a CEO, or any leader, become more self-aware. As Kouzes and Posner

The Leadership Challenge, Fifth Edition by James M. Kouzes and Barry Z. Posner, Copyright © 2012 All rights reserved. Published by Jossey-Bass, A Wiley Imprint. www.josseybass.com

say, *"There is solid evidence that the best leaders are highly attuned to what's going on inside themselves as they are leading, and to what's going on with others. They're very self-aware, and they're very socially aware."*

This questionnaire—which can be found in the Appendix on page 185—is based on the "Five Practices of Exemplary Leadership" their research uncovered. They found that the high performers were "best in class" in these five areas:

1. They Modeled the Way
2. Inspired a Shared Vision
3. Challenged the Process
4. Enabled Others to Act
5. Encouraged the Heart

The LPI gives leaders feedback on how the important people around them feel they are doing, versus their own perception, in these five leadership areas.

It is extremely valuable feedback. The key is not trying to improve everything at once. Tackle one thing at a time and make it better.

If you haven't received 360-degree feedback on your leadership in the past year, I recommend you do. It will pay great dividends for you and your team.

TOOL—THE ED RYAN MAGIC: GETTING THE A PLAYERS

Ed Ryan started MPR in 1976 on the ideology that "the

most critical ingredient for the survival and growth of any organization is talented personnel."

As Ed always says, *"CEOs should not be in the behavior modification business. Find people with the traits you need to achieve your vision."* He believes that behaviors predict success more than experience. He urges CEOs to focus on behavior selection versus behavior modification. Great advice. How much time do CEOs waste trying to change someone's behavior? Too much.

Remember the number one trait of A players is resourcefulness—the ability to get things done!

Ed listens for this trait, along with other traits identified as being critical to the candidate's success, in a two-to-three-hour interview. He listens between the lines. He is a master at it.

I am a strong advocate for Ed because I have used his system and it works.

Ed's system is based on the following ideas:

- Behaviors, more than experience, will predict success
- Experience is only one dimension of a person's profile and it is often the least predictive of his or her fit or success
- Practice behavior selection not behavior modification
- Identify and choose those individuals who can

deliver the behaviors needed to successfully perform in a given role

- Evaluate and select the whole person
- Hire slowly and fire quickly
- Hastily made hiring and promotion decisions usually lead to problems later that a more deliberate, thorough process up-front would undoubtedly avoid

Ed evaluates three dimensions of a person when considering a candidate's suitability:

- **Behavioral Traits:** the behaviors required to perform the job
- **Experience:** the education and job-related experience that contribute to quicker productivity
- **Chemistry:** the factors of corporate culture, management style, and team dynamics

The number one differentiator between my business and the other guys is the quality of our CEO Group Leaders. Every candidate I consider for group leadership must pass the Ed Ryan test to have a chance.

Ed forces me to really think through the most important traits I look for in our Group Leaders by having me select my five top Group Leader traits from the following list:

MOTIVATIONS

Achiever
Competitor

Mission of Service
Producer
Responsibility

MODES OF THINKING

Discerner
Self-Awareness
Pragmatic Intelligence
Innovator
Values

MODES OF ACTING

Intensity
Proactively
Strategist
Technical Mastery

MODES OF INTERACTING

Assertor
Communicator
Empathy
Persuader
Relator

For the record, these are the top five traits from the list that I look for in our CEO Group Leaders:

- Achiever
- Mission of Service
- Discerner

- Empathy
- Relator

These are the non-negotiables for me.

Each CEO Group Leader candidate has a two-to-three-hour phone interview with one of Ed's people, with the interviewer asking questions and recording the candidate's answers. Ed and his team listen to the answers.

They are looking for hard evidence of the traits I need to have a team of outstanding CEO Group Leaders. Every time they hear a trait they make a check mark. At the end, they add it all up and grade each trait on a scale of one to ten.

I receive a one pager on each candidate showing me where they score on that one-to-ten scale for each of the 18 traits and, most importantly, on the top five traits I am looking for in our CEO Group Leaders. I have included the results of my benchmark MPR test in the Appendix on page 183.

It is an excellent system.

I recommend it.

TOOL—BEST PERFORMANCE MANAGEMENT SYSTEM: CATALYTIC COACHING

There are many performance management systems available that utilize quality feedback to enhance performance, but my favorite was invented by Garold (Gary) Markle. Gary is on a personal mission to do away with what he refers to as "the world's poorest performing personnel practice—the performance evaluation." In its place, he's designed a less taxing and much more positive program that employees embrace and appreciate, and managers don't consider a big waste of time. His system is the best I have ever seen.

Gary is the founder and managing principal of Energage Inc., a consulting firm dedicated to helping business leaders. Gary and his associates have assisted companies throughout the United States and Canada in forming and improving their people-development systems.

In his book, *Catalytic Coaching: The End of the Performance Review*, Gary clearly outlines the case against traditional performance evaluation systems and advocates a much more effective coaching-based option.

Step 1. Your direct report completes the Coaching Input Sheet where he or she answers these questions:

- What have I done for the company lately?:
  What are my accomplishments? (What I set out to do and did.)
  What are my disappointments? (What I set out to do and didn't.)

- What have I done for myself lately?
  This speaks to personal growth: new skills acquired, important experiences gained, or relationships built that make me more productive. It also implies something about career ownership. The intent of Catalytic Coaching is for employees to be in charge of their own career development.

Catalytic Coaching: The End of the Performance Review by Garold L. Markle, Copyright © 2000 Garold L. Markle. All rights reserved. Published by Quorum Books. www.energage.com

The leader, as coach, guides and assists.

- What would I like to do when I grow up?
  In one to two years?
  Five years?
  Ultimately?

- What are other important things you should
  know as my coach?

This is followed by a 45-minute to one-hour presentation of responses by your direct reports to you. They talk—you listen.

Step 2. You complete the Catalytic Coaching Worksheet in which you:

- Outline their top strengths
- Outline their areas of improvement and whether they are performance impacting, potential enhancing, or job threatening
- Make your development recommendations

This is followed by another 45-minute to one-hour meeting. This time, you talk—they listen.

Step 3. Your Direct Reports complete the Personal Development Plan:

This third meeting takes an average of 15 minutes wherein the employee lays out an action plan to address no more than four "Areas for Improvement" from the Catalytic Coaching Worksheet.

Step 4. You monitor the progress of the Personal Development Plan during 15-minute meetings conducted quarterly.

It works outstandingly well.

Here's why.

It is future-focused and clearly defines and prioritizes the desired business outcomes. The leader becomes a coach rather than an evaluator or judge. It also breaks the ties between performance and salary administration.

Go ahead ... blow up your performance evaluation process. In my experience, Catalytic Coaching dramatically outperforms the traditional performance management systems.

Examples of a Catalytic Coaching Input Sheet, a Coaching Worksheet, and a Personal Development Plan can be found in the Appendix, beginning on page 178. You can also learn more about Catalytic Coaching on Gary's website at www.energage.com.

TOOL—ACCOUNTABILITY AND ALIGNMENT: QPM

Some of the finest lessons I have ever learned on accountability come from the great Kraig Kramers.

The best idea is simply called QPM, which stands for Quarterly Priorities Management. Kraig rates QPM as the *"very best self-accountability tool"* he has ever seen. For what it's worth, so do I. QPM is also an excellent tool for achieving alignment on your strategic plan.

He believes that the secret to organizing others is to help your team members develop self-accountability. Kraig insists that QPM is the single most powerful management tool that keeps CEOs and their top management team focused on the right stuff.

Here is how it works:

First, you identify your top five goals or priorities. These are the top five things you must achieve over the next 90 days to achieve your three- or five-year strategic plan. As Kraig says, *"As CEO, your focus on the long-term vision needs to be translated into how you will get from here to there for everyone in the company."* The question is—what are the five big things you need to focus on for the next 90 days to get you closer to your vision? Focus on the big, important stuff.

Now, cascade that QPM down to all of your direct reports. Just think. If you have six direct reports on your senior team, and all of them focus on their five big things and know clearly what yours are, when you have your team meetings you will be able to get a status report on the top 30 quarterly priorities for your company. That is accountability. It begins with clarity. Hold people accountable on the top five things that they are doing to achieve the strategic plan.

That's how you beat the competition. It is simply the most effective tool to ensure you and your team are on the same page. Just think ... you will have your team's top priorities to achieve your vision at your fingertips.

The great thing about Kraig is that he has been there, done that. He is a successful CEO and has turned around many companies including Snapper, Guarantee Insurance, Metro-One Telecommunications, Courtesy Coffee, Munson Sporting Goods, and Graphic Arts Center.

Oh, and by the way, he is also a "rocket scientist," having his BS in physics from MIT and an MBA in marketing and finance from Stanford University. Two pretty good schools.

If you haven't read his book, I recommend you do.

TOOL—FIERCE CONVERSATIONS: THE CONFRONTATIONAL MODEL

Leaders often put off making tough decisions because that can mean dealing with confrontation. And what CEO seeks out confrontation?

Great CEOs deal with conflict. They don't sweep it under the rug or avoid it; they face it and look it straight in the eye. They deal with it.

One of Patrick Lencioni's *Five Temptations of a CEO* is the avoidance of conflict; meaning choosing harmony over productive conflict. One of his *Five Dysfunctions of a Team* is the fear of conflict. As he calls it, the desire to preserve harmony stifles the occurrence of productive, ideological conflict.

Susan Scott taught me the best tool I have ever seen for meeting conflict head-on. Susan is the master of "fierce conversations" and knows so much about dealing with conflict that she wrote one of the best books ever written on the topic of real, authentic conversations. Her *Fierce Conversations: Achieving Success at Work & in Life, One Conversation at a Time* is a must-read for every CEO.

Several years ago, I had the privilege of learning from Susan at her two-day Fierce Conversations Workshop in Lake Las Vegas. Role-play after role-play after role-play on the most difficult conversations I had been avoiding.

I suffer from Patrick Lencioni's popularity temptation.

Susan helped me with that. Her Confrontational Model is brilliant and a great tool for CEOs.

I still want to be popular, but I will have that fierce conversation. I don't avoid it like I did before meeting Susan.

Thanks to Susan, I have a model that gives me the confidence and yes, the courage, to confront the tough issues. By role-playing an upcoming confrontational conversation with my mentor, I ensure that relationships are enriched by the learning gained from the fierce conversations I have with others.

By the way, fierce means real, genuine, and authentic.

Susan believes that relationships are made or destroyed one conversation at a time. How true is that! I never thought of it that way until I heard Susan say it.

Step one is the opening statement. This is a 60-second or less sentence or two that addresses "why we are having this conversation." It is critical step to the success of the conversation, and is the absolute most important piece in Susan's model to me. Why? Because it all starts there. It puts the ball in play and you want it straight down the middle. You need to write it down, then rewrite it, and rewrite it. It is vital to get it right. You have no idea how many times I rewrote mine to get it right. Then I practiced by saying it out loud. Time and time again.

"My Group Leader probes so that the answer presents itself on its own. He asks tough questions to help me narrow in on a potential solution. We went into role-playing and worked out how to characterize the issue, how to present it in a way that others would see it in the way that I wanted them to rather than it being received incorrectly. We just hit it from 12 sides, so that when I was in the position to have that conversation, it was a home run. It was that simple."

~ Chris Gower, Executive Vice President of PCL
Constructors Canada Inc.

The opening statement names the issue, gives an example illustrating the behavior I want changed, describes my emotions on the issue, states clearly what is at stake, identifies my fingerprints on the problem, and states clearly that I want the issue resolved.

Then I invite the person to respond. All that in 60 seconds or less.

In step two I listen and ask clarifying questions. I want to be sure I fully understand and acknowledge their position.

In step three, I clearly define what is needed for resolution.

In step four, we make a new agreement and decide how we will hold each other responsible for making sure the new agreement is kept.

Four simple steps in a model designed to help CEOs have the fierce conversations that perhaps have been avoided for too long. Remember Joe and the gold watch? Susan's Confrontational Model helps weed out the "Joes" and helps CEOs build their A team.

CEO Action Items to Dramatically Improve Your Company's Performance

1. Use the Hartman KPI Template and Kraig Kramers' T12M charts as a financial dashboard

2. Complete a CEO Report Card

3. Complete a Leadership 360 and work on the biggest gap

4. Implement a Behavior Benchmark program for hiring

5. Read *Catalytic Coaching: The End of the Performance Review* by Gary Markle and implement Catalytic Coaching

6. Implement Quarterly Priorities Management to keep you and your team focused on the right stuff

7. Read Susan Scott's *Fierce Conversations*— and have the one you are avoiding

Chapter Six

Perfect Balance:
The Work–Life Question

"One of the main implications of being out of balance, however you define it, is that you neglect other areas of your life; family, health, etc., are often some of the first. When you become so addicted to only dealing with your urgent tasks you don't think there is time for the non-urgent. By the time these things become urgent, it's often too late to affect them."

~ Stephen R. Covey, author of *The 7 Habits of Highly Effective People*®

Twenty years ago, when my family was based in California, I started a company with some partners and was having a lot of fun building the business.

Selfishly, I became one of those 24/7 businesspeople. I did an awful lot of traveling, which was very tough on my wife, Lynne, and our young daughter, Jen. I was fortunate in that it did not pull my family apart. But many others are not so lucky.

Great CEOs strive to make the right moves to ensure their life has balance and they live life to its fullest. Their focus is not just business, not just on increasing their net worth, not on just climbing to the top of the corporate ladder.

I know CEOs who have found balance through a triggering event—a jolt of reality: coming home from a business trip and finding their wife and kids have moved out; having a heart attack; losing relationships with family and friends that were at one time so important; losing the company; losing their way.

I know CEOs who haven't found balance because of guilt, lack of confidence, lack of clarity, lack of a sensible plan, lack of a good team, an absence of any other place to be or any other passion.

But Great CEOs do find balance. Great CEOs do not need to be workaholics!

Great CEOs figure this out. They have a peer group of

CEOs to help them find their way.

Steve Hartman also had his Dad.

FINDING BALANCE

Steve Hartman is the leader of a very successful company. As the CEO/Owner of Industrial Thermo Polymers (ITP) Ltd., Steve has figured it out. He epitomizes the leader who understands the necessity of having good people around him in order to achieve balance.

Steve and his Dad started ITP over 30 years ago, and it is now a leading international manufacturer of extruded polyethylene foam products in North America.

Here is what Steve has to say about the importance of balance:

My Dad taught me that the company is here to serve us, not the other way around. You don't have to spend a hundred hours a week running it if you run it properly. Bring in the people to do the jobs you can't do. Recognize you can't be good at everything. CEOs should download what they are not good at and focus on what they are good at. The business is there to make you happy, not the other way around.

Dean Martin figured it out a different way. Dean is the owner of Melmart Distributors Inc. Melmart is a leading flooring distributor within the markets it has served for almost 45 years.

My father was a workaholic. He worked 12 to 15 hours a day. When I was 18, he died unexpectedly in his sleep at age 60. I am the youngest of six, and for a long time there was resentment toward him for the time he spent at the office instead of being at home with his kids.

I learned how to work by observing and following my father's example. When I took over the company, I ran all over the place, working 12 hours or more a day, absolutely convinced that this is what I had to do.

I can remember calling my wife at midnight and saying, "The computer is still not working right. I'm not leaving until it is so the company will be up and running in the morning."

I also felt like I had to set an example for the employees. The problem was I became stressed out.

Today, Dean is totally on top of his game. He is still a Great CEO but no longer a workaholic.

He has found balance in his life. He found a way to not feel guilty when he wasn't at the office. He lost the need to be at the office longer than anyone to set an example for the employees.

His business is a success and his personal life is a success. He takes four to six weeks of vacation with his family each year, and is very involved with making his community, and his country, better through a number of church and charitable activities. He is an outstanding role model for other CEOs seeking work–life balance.

"As I've gotten older (and hopefully a little wiser), I have realized the need to be careful and put in the required time on all three areas: work, family, and self. I also now know not to ever take any of these for granted. All these areas are interconnected, and you must be prepared to give a lot. It's not about being a workaholic, but hard work is part of it. I have seen, and lived both sides of this 'balance,' sometimes more successfully than others. It will always be a challenge but too many guys end up with a ton of business success and a personal life in shambles. Conversely, it is just a simple reality that in order to do the job well at work, there will be times it will take a toll at home. Having a spouse who understands this is a big part of it, and I am incredibly blessed in both cases."

~ Grant Heggie, President and CEO, Melmart Distributors

How did he get there? He made two important business decisions.

First, he hired an A player to be his president and CEO. Grant Heggie is someone Dean trusts totally.

Second, Dean meets monthly with his CEO peer group and Group Leader, who "check his backswing" and hold him accountable on the things that are important in his life.

Here are some insights on balance from two members of Dean's CEO peer group:

Chris Gower, Executive Vice President of PCL Constructors Canada Inc., explains that *"One of the greatest experiences with our CEO peer group, which you don't always get at work, is learning how to balance career with family. I got to know myself better. I became more attentive to my wife and kids. I brought less work home and became less self-absorbed. My wife and I now have conversations that are far less about work. I have also made time for my son and daughter. I'm not saying I'm perfect. I'm no less driven or focused at work. But I'm just more balanced in my approach. It's now about 'us,' not just about me."*

Michael Burrows, CEO of Maple Lodge Farms, points out that *"Each of us has multiple roles, defining who we are. We have our business life, personal life, and family life. It's a challenge for a CEO to find balance in that equation. But being able to be effective in each of those areas has a huge impact on your ability to be the best you can be in general. If your family life is a mess, for example, I couldn't imagine how it would not affect your business life."*

WHAT DO YOU WANT FROM YOUR LIFE?

It helps to know what you want from your life. Take time to figure out that important question. What do you want to do with the rest of your life? What are the most important things for you? Who and what do you love the most?

Dale Armstrong figured it out. Dale is the CEO and owner of the highly successful Armstrong International Ltd.

The first time I met Dale he told me that unless he could figure out a way to run his business two days a week, he would throw the keys inside the front door and walk away. Getting balance in his life was that important to him. He knew what he wanted and it wasn't working five days a week. He wanted to spend quality time with his wife and their children and travel the world. He was a man on a mission.

He said, *"Help me find a way to accomplish more in 40 percent of the time ... two days a week instead of five."*

The key is spending time on the right stuff with the right team.

Dale did that.

He joined a CEO peer group and met with them every month. He quickly established a reputation as the guy who "gets things done" as he devoured the lessons learned at his group meetings. He quickly implemented the new learning he gained from Susan Scott's *Fierce Conversations* and Kraig Kramers' *CEO Tools*. In fact, every CEO meeting Dale attends; every speaker he hears; every business book he reads; he makes sure he takes away at least one good idea, and executes it to make his business better.

Dale was able to achieve his goal of accomplishing more in two days by leveraging his time with new ideas he learned from other CEOs.

Dale works on the important not the urgent. Works on the business—not in it.

He has a clear vision for the business and has developed an excellent team to successfully implement the strategies to achieve the vision.

Dale places a high value on his time and as a result, does not waste it. He was a man in a hurry. In a hurry to spend time on the things he values the most; the people he loves. Now he is able to!

THE DEREK BULLEN STORY

For me, one of the best authorities on getting the work–life balance right is Derek Bullen, CEO and owner of S.i. Systems Ltd., headquartered in Calgary, Alberta. I first read about Derek in *Profit$ Magazine* in March 2003. The headline read: "Perfect Balance." It caught my eye.

It was the story of Derek's business and personal journey to find the real purpose of his life. To find the perfect balance.

For a workaholic running a business that was going nowhere fast this was a big challenge. Derek met it.

The article began with the phrase "work is life," which was Derek's old motto. His schedule was one of perpetual motion. Eighty-hour work weeks were his standard. Work was constantly on his mind. Stressed out; his family came last. As Derek said, *"I wasn't spending any time with my family and I wasn't making any money. My company was just wallowing."*

That was 1995. Eight years later, Derek had figured it out with the help of his mentor and CEO peer group and was working just 40 hours a week, taking two months' vacation, and still running one of Canada's fastest growing companies.

When I read about Derek's amazing journey of self-discovery and personal growth I gave him a call to ask if he would speak to the CEOs I work with. He agreed.

His story is inspiring. How did such a workaholic find balance?

Derek's way was through faith and spirituality. When you meet him you know he has developed a strong self-awareness, his purpose in life, and his place in the world.

This clarity helped him re-evaluate his purpose and find passion, confidence, and inner peace in all aspects of his life.

Derek says that *"the toughest thing when you change yourself is to let go of your fears. You have to have faith to let go."* He discovered that time off exposed him to new ideas. *"Taking time off allows you space to let the big ideas in."*

I have heard Derek speak to CEO groups a number of times. He starts by asking each person how long they think they will live. It is a great question because it quickly brings into focus the value of time and the value of life.

It quickly gets the CEOs to a discussion of how they will spend the remaining years of their life.

Derek then has the CEOs look at some of the big options available for their time: the business, the community, health, family, friends, learning, travel, self-discovery, charities, spirituality, quiet time for self ... so many choices ... so little time.

The amazing thing is, the more time Derek spent on the non-business aspects of his life, the more successful his business became!

His personal growth journey included spending four days without food and water at the foot of the Rockies under the supervision of the Kainai (Blood Tribe) First Nation. He came away from that experience with two revelations—to spend more time with his children and to take more personal time.

Derek has also completed a seven-day walking trek across northern Spain to a cathedral in Santiago de Compostela, and has worked feeding the poor with Mother Teresa in Calcutta. And every summer he takes a month with his family and lives in a different part of the world.

I asked Derek to show the CEOs a chart tracking the milestones of his personal growth journey with the growth of his company. They tracked very closely and both took off like a rocket. This chart can be viewed on page 130.

Here's the lesson: Derek believes that if he hadn't grown personally, his firm would not have prospered.

THE PRICE OF IMBALANCE

What many CEOs fail to realize is the price that has to be paid for too much work. Study after study has shown that a working life out of balance is less healthy, less happy, and—most importantly—less productive than its opposite. And since the success of the company largely depends on its CEO, a healthy and happy CEO is vital to overall performance.

Some studies have suggested that executives' performance can decrease by as much as 25 percent when they work in excess of 60 hours per week for prolonged periods. Physical and mental fatigue leads to slower work, more mistakes, and wasted time.

Lisa MacNeil is an outstanding leader with Gordon Food Service Ltd. Like most leaders, Lisa has struggled with finding "the perfect balance." Her comments speak well to the importance of finding it.

I was often stressed by work. The team looked at me as someone who never sat down, never stopped, and was always driving forward. My work–life balance scale was malfunctioning.

As a result of listening to other members in my peer group, I learned to be the calm in the storm. By implementing some of their suggestions, I became less stressed, less judgmental, and more reflective. I am not sure you ever find complete balance in your life, but by having them there to hold me accountable, I now spend more quality time with my husband and kids. I would like to be remembered as a good leader but also a great person, wife, and mother.

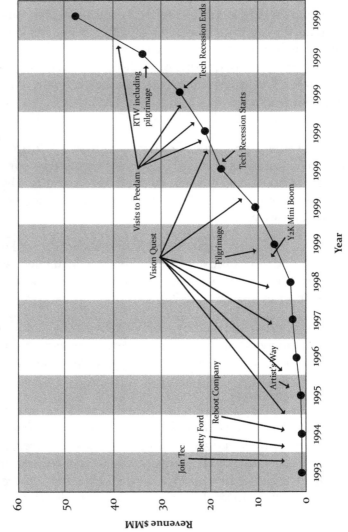

S.i. Systems Ltd. 10 Year Revenue History

DIFFERENT STROKES

Carolyn Robertson asks CEOs a great question: "Why do you think you are here on this earth?" Certainly not an easy question to answer but one that fosters discussion and helps bring clarity of purpose and priorities, and it is the engine to finding the "Perfect Balance."

Every person has a different answer to Carolyn's question. Not everyone wants to work only two days a week. Not everyone wants to walk a pilgrimage in Spain or climb Mount Everest.

At a meeting several years ago, 14 CEOs were quite unexpectedly drawn into a discussion on work–life balance. One of them said that success for him was only working three days a week and that if anyone around the table hadn't achieved that level of freedom then they weren't leading right.

That set off a very spirited discussion on "what's right for you isn't necessarily right for me." Some said they enjoyed being at their business every day. They loved their business and wanted to continue to build it at a fast pace. Others felt they did need to recalibrate and pay more attention to other aspects of their lives. Some wanted to ramp up the spiritual, others wanted to give more of themselves to their communities and others wanted to strengthen some important relationships.

In my experience, I have found that the "Perfect Balance" ebbs and flows through life. There are times when I have found the "zone"—that place where everything seems to flow and life seems effortless. That is the perfect balance for me. Blurring the lines between work and play. Spending time on the things that bring the most pleasure to life.

There is no magic formula for achieving a work–life balance. What it means and how it's achieved is different for everyone. That's because it's specific to the individual; what works for one person may not work for another. And it will change as your personal life and career evolve. It's not simply a matter of taking time off either. It's a combination of activities, either at or outside of work, provided they are "not work," that allow one to achieve health, happiness, and optimum productivity. Carolyn's big question helps you drill down to the answer for you.

Don't answer it on the run. Take a long time out to give the question the attention it deserves.

Great CEOs find the "Perfect Balance" for their life and the lives of the ones they love.

CEO Action Items to Achieve Your Perfect Balance

1. Ensure that you have an A team in place (see Chapter 3)

2. Work *on* your business more, and *in it* less

3. Answer the question: What do you want from your life?

4. Take time out to "let the big ideas in" and determine your life's purpose

5. Based on your life's purpose, identify *your* Perfect Balance role model

6. Develop a plan to achieve your life's purpose

7. Think Dale Armstrong and Derek Bullen— execute your plan to achieve your life's purpose

Chapter Seven

The CEO Connection:
Be Lonely No More!

*"The opportunity to talk to other presidents
and to share with outside people who
understand your reality—to have their advice
and their experience—is really useful. It can
get lonely at the top. It's nice to have a place
where you can bounce ideas around and
hear about others' lives, the decisions they
made, and learn from them."*

~ Anne Martin, CEO, United Van Lines

Many CEOs and senior leaders suffer from what Daniel Goleman calls the "CEO Disease." As he explains in his book *Primal Leadership*, these people rarely hear the truth.

Not from their management team, their employees, their board, their shareholders, their suppliers, their customers, or their competitors. According to Goleman, the CEO Disease is *"fed by the natural instinct to please the boss, resulting in a widespread tendency to give positive feedback and withhold the negative whenever information flows upward."*

"You need an opportunity to talk about the things that you are struggling with, that you haven't been able to get in the right place. Things that come across my desk usually are the complex, difficult things. To have an external, unbiased resource of quality people to bounce ideas off of, explain problems to, and get feedback from is a very good thing."

~ Jim Greenwood, retired head of Gordon Food Service Canada Company Inc., and former CEO and owner of Finlay Greenwood

---

Compliments, complaints, and criticisms can have a hidden agenda. Comments are measured; punches are pulled.

All your jokes are funny.

This is one of the reasons it can feel lonely at the top. Who do you turn to? Who can you talk to and receive honest and productive feedback?

LONELY AT THE TOP

Lonely at the top? Sometimes the top can feel like the bottom. I hit bottom at a Fairfield Inn in Dallas, Texas, circa 1995. I was CEO/Owner of a rapidly growing fleet fueling company at the time. Cash never flows fast enough when you need it. And did I ever need it. Suppliers insisting on payment before they would release the next load of gasoline for our stations, too many customers were dragging out their payments, and the employees who remained needed to get paid so they could pay their bills and put food on their tables.

I will never forget the fear that gripped me. The feeling cannot be put into words. The pressure that kept increasing until I felt I was going to explode. How am I going to meet payroll this afternoon? They never talked about this unending, relentless pressure at business school. When is the next call with more bad news? What are my options? Who do I turn to? Who do I call? What do I say? What is the next surprise? How did I get here?

There was absolutely no one I could talk to about these pressures!

I don't want any CEOs to ever have to go through what I went through.

Be clear; there is absolutely no need to be lonely. Be lonely no more.

CEOs helping CEOs succeed. That is what CEO peer groups are all about. Helping CEOs not go to these lonely, painful places.

Get involved with a group of non-competing CEOs, none of whom are your major customers or major suppliers. Find a group of CEOs who will tell you the unfiltered, unmeasured truth. Find a group of CEOs who stand for your success.

"One of the interesting things, for me, is that we're a mid-range company, but there are people in my CEO peer group who do billions of dollars in sales. And so you would never have the opportunity or the access to them; they're just too busy. So to have access to 16 of them in your meetings, or even at a quarterly dinner where there are 200 people is amazing."

~ Anne Martin, CEO, United Van Lines, Canada's largest network of moving companies and the winner of multiple third-party awards, including Canada's *50 Best Managed Companies* award for three years running.

Initially a group of strangers; these CEOs will become your confidants, your sounding board. You will learn to trust them and they to trust you. They will care for you and you for them. Everything you discuss will be kept in the strictest confidence. Confidentiality and trust are the cornerstones for a successful CEO Group.

It has been proven that when CEOs are suffering from personal problems, the effect of support from family and friends is 53 percent to 79 percent weaker than support from fellow CEOs in restoring the leaders' overall effectiveness.

Michael Burrows, CEO of Maple Lodge Farms, understands the value of CEO peer groups:

As a CEO, you can become isolated or insulated, while the world, its expectation, and your responsibilities continue to change around you.

If you are not exposed to new things and different ways of thinking, you will gradually fall behind. You have to evolve as you move the business forward. It is critical to find opportunities to get new learning and connect with people who can bring you different experiences and insights.

Mentoring from a CEO peer group is a critical part of this learning. CEOs have so many challenges in common. Just because somebody is in an entirely different industry doesn't mean that you can't learn from them. It is quite the opposite. It's their perspective that opens your mind. Having exposure to lots of different industries and companies, you gain great ideas on how to increase your company's success.

The relevance of our expertise in a particular industry

is becoming less meaningful. It is our leadership experiences and the degree that we can transfer those skills, practices, and knowledge that's key.

That is what my CEO peer group has taught me. The feedback, mentoring, and broad-based CEO insights have been of great benefit. My CEO peer group will not make me a more expert food industry executive, but it will make me a "more expert" CEO, and being a more expert leader and CEO brings lots of value to an organization, its employees, and their families, suppliers, communities, and shareholders.

Steve Gallant, Managing Partner of Accucam Machining agrees, adding, *"Recently, as a manufacturing company, we experienced a business environment that was extraordinarily negative. While working to navigate these unexpected events and circumstances, I received outstanding support, counsel, and good advice from my CEO peer group and Group Leader. As a result of the conversations and positive ideas generated during the meetings and open discussions with the group we were able to make the adjustments necessary. Most importantly, my membership in my CEO peer group made me realize that I was not alone."*

Make it real; hear the truth from CEOs who care for you. Learn from them.

Imagine a window into how other successful CEOs run their companies and how they run their lives; a window into their minds and their industries; their opportunities and challenges. That is powerful learning for any CEO.

You will find that what keeps them up at night is exactly

The CEO Connection: Be Lonely No More!

the same stuff that keeps you up at night: people, cash flow, growth, EBITDA, competitors, health, relationships, poor performers, high performers, the dollar, the economy, share price, the government, finding and keeping top talent, leading change, inspiring people, and inspiring self.

At the top, every leader's opportunities and challenges are the same. A hundred percent commonality.

CONTINUOUS LEARNING

Steve Jobs, during a commencement address to Stanford MBA graduates, closed his remarks by asking them to "Stay Hungry." As the CEO of your company you have to "Stay Learning." So you can beat the competition. Win the day.

Great CEOs are always learning. They are made and remade and remade by learning and particularly learning from other CEOs.

"That transition from manager to executive may seem small in the eyes of many, but everything changes for you—the pressure, responsibility, scheduling, relationships with employees, and even family life. I had heard about those things, but never imagined the transition would impact my life the way it eventually did. I needed a way

141

to make sure I was adapting to the changes and staying on track. My company, family, and job depended on it.

Before I joined, I worried about spending that half day each month not at my desk or in other important meetings. I now look forward to that day, and even schedule trips around it. The chance for me to openly discuss the challenges I'm facing is something I can't get anywhere else. More importantly, the opportunity to get honest feedback from a dozen other business leaders is invaluable. I've made some of the most important decisions of my life with the help of my CEO peer group.

"The most important thing is that you're with other leaders and so you're with a group of people who are going through exactly the same things you are. You're getting unfiltered information on things that others have experienced already."

~ Rick Morris, President, Construction Specialties Co.

There is no better way for CEOs to get on top of their game and stay there than meeting regularly with a group of CEOs who will tell them the truth and, because of the trust in the room, share their most effective best practices to help every other CEO succeed.

To learn from an elite, private brain trust that stands for your success is powerful.

"To get the most out of a CEO peer group, and learn how to make the tough decisions, you have to be honest about your business; bring out your most sensitive issues and hard facts and put them on the table."

~ William Tharp, CEO, The Climate Change Infrastructure Corporation

---

The number one way that Great CEOs learn is from other successful CEOs! From a CEO peer group. A CEO network!

Paul Rockett, founder and CEO of Sherway Group, says:

"The number one reason I am in a CEO Group is to learn from other CEOs. I have learned to make my company more successful. It is much more stable now.

I feel very fortunate. Every month at our CEO meeting, I am in a room with such dynamic players ... some of these guys are leading billion-dollar companies.

I know I have been successful but, when some of those guys talk, you can't take enough of it in. Being part of such a dynamic group of CEOs has been a tremendous thing for me."

Roger Grochmal, CEO/Owner of AtlasCare, agrees: *"As the CEO, you need to be doing something to increase your knowledge base every day. As leaders we can be so engaged with the running and execution phase of the business that we are not actively learning. By being with other CEOs, the learning is phenomenal."*

Jamie Moody, the CEO of Tree of Life Canada, certainly saw the power in the CEO brain trust: *"I was a brand new CEO, had been general manager and senior VP, and gone up through the ranks and ran functional silos before. Then, when I had the chance to lead the entire organization, I knew I needed to get myself the right CEO support network to enable me to learn from others and improve my chances of success."*

Jamie and his team have certainly done that; they hit the ball out of the park year after year with their financial performance. They truly outperform their competition.

And Bill Kooy, the president and CEO of Kooy Brothers, the very successful snow plow and lawn equipment company, says, *"By learning some very simple things from other CEOs in my Group, I have been able to reduce my anxiety level dramatically. It turned my world around completely. I feel so much better about the business and have a more thorough understanding of the issues swirling around me.*

We have had dramatic growth over the past nine years."

A CEO peer group gives you a place to bring your biggest decisions; the big opportunities that can take your company to greater heights if you are right or take you down if you are wrong.

You don't have to make these decisions alone. Take them to your CEO brain trust and get their honest feedback on what they feel is the right decision.

That is just what Marcia Mayhew did. At the time, she was the incoming CEO of Mayhew, a company that had been in her family for four generations. A company founded by her great-grandmother.

In my first year as a young and green CEO, there were many big decisions to make. People were looking to me for all the answers. Yet, I felt I often didn't have answers to even some of the most basic questions within my business. I needed a confidant to whom I could speak with candor. I also needed a sounding board to give me honest feedback. In the role of CEO, you tend to hear what you want to hear versus what you need to hear. In my CEO Group, they tell me what I need to hear because they truly care about my success and have no other agenda. When I first joined my CEO Group, I was asked to present my company's Key Performance Indicators. The Group challenged me and made me aware that I needed more than a couple of historical references to run the business. They taught me that I can't make good decisions and run my company blind. Because of them standing for my success and openly sharing their experiences and generously giving me frank, timely, and high quality feedback, I realized that I had a group of CEOs watching out for me, walking beside me. They had my back. With their support, we have structured our business for growth, and the future for our business looks even better.

Mayhew & Associates was recognized as one of *Canada's Best Managed Companies* and one of *The Achievers 50 Most Engaged Workplaces*™ in 2011. Says Marcia, *"I attribute much of my external recognition to the positive changes I made with Mayhew due to my involvement with [my CEO peer group] over the past two and a half years."*

So, just what exactly happens on that day when these CEOs come together? Magic, that's what happens. Something very special.

The common characteristic in every one of these CEOs is that they are lifelong learners. People who want to keep learning so they can be the best they can be at what they do—lead others, inspire others, build companies.

Another critical dimension of CEO learning is to stay curious; ask smart questions; listen carefully. As Naseem Somani, the CEO of Gamma-Dynacare says, *"the successful CEO must ask very good questions in order to get at the root causes of issues and enable rapid rectification."*

THE MENTOR BENEFIT

Another way that Great CEOs get better at their craft and stay on top of their game is to have an outstanding CEO Group Leader as a mentor. The learning that CEOs gain from their CEO Group Leader is powerful.

"I worked alongside my Dad for 22 years. We were equal shareholders from day one, so we had to agree on things before we did them. If one of us said no you were at an impasse. After my Dad's death I needed a new sounding board. I joined a CEO peer group and started listening to other CEOs talk, people with experience that I didn't have. You pick out the bits that apply to your business and implement them.

When you lose a partner, and all of a sudden you don't have that person you can just bounce ideas off, you feel a bit lost. I had the help of my peer group to provide me feedback and act as a sounding board. My CEO Group is a group of friends, but friends that understand business from a CEO perspective."

~ Steve Hartman, founder and CEO of Industrial Thermo Polymers Ltd.

Here's a thought from David Dobbin regarding the value of having a CEO Group Leader as a mentor:

My Group Leader acts very much like my business conscience. A lot of times I find that I know what the right an-

swer is, but I don't want to do it for some reason, or I'm hesitating or simply being lazy. They help keep me honest.

As I reflect on my executive development experience, I spend more time thinking about the impact of my leadership and the decisions I make, and the things I put in place and how it's going to. The full ripple effect is in view for me now. I think a lot more than I used to before I did this.

I think a lot more about the impact on people and their families from decisions that I make, and how I conduct myself as a person and leader. I believe my family would say I'm more concerned with the long term than I used to be.

"Successful leaders typically make a significant investment in developing relationships with a set of external peers. This is critically important for leaders of smaller organizations as well as those in larger ones. CEO organizations give you access to a large network and the opportunity to become a member in a small inner-circle thinking group."

~ Saj-nicole A. Joni, PhD, author of *The Third Opinion: How Successful Leaders Use Outside Insight to Create Superior Results*

Saj-nicole A. Joni, PhD, wrote a great book titled *The Third Opinion: How Successful Leaders Use Outside Insight to*

Create Superior Results. Joni is the founder of Cambridge International Groups Ltd., a high-level advisory services firm and she is widely regarded as one of the leading third-opinion advisors to executives around the world.

In her book, she states that *"leadership in the modern era demands external thinking partners in addition to a top-notch internal team."* She also says that *"To be a successful leader today you need, perhaps above all, to know your own limits. And then, you need to know how to go out and find others who can take you the rest of the way."*

Finding the right CEO peer group can "take you the rest of the way." Joni encourages leaders to *"accelerate your own development from the lessons of others."* How intelligent is that? Great CEOs do it!

She also talks about how *"isolation limits your effectiveness, leaving you trying to manage the complexity without the resources you need."* And that, *"the greater your responsibilities, the more imperative it is that you talk with others."*

As Joni says, *"No matter how skilled, dedicated, and intelligent you are, you can't know what you don't know. Ensure that you leave no stone unturned, that all relevant questions are asked, that data is vetted for bias, and that all the possible interdependencies are considered."*

She is absolutely right-on when she says that these thinking partners will *"expand the edge of your own comfort zone by exploring the unvarnished truth."* Your CEO Group Leaders will *"push you and they will have the ability and the willingness to ask, not just the unasked questions, but, when needed, the unaskable questions."*

"In the role of CEO, you tend to hear what you want to hear versus what you need to hear. In my CEO Group, they tell me what I need to hear because they truly care about my success and have no other agenda."

~ Marcia Mayhew, CEO, Mayhew & Associates

To be a great CEO Group Leader you need to have a big heart; that is the number one quality of a successful mentor. You really want to help others succeed. Ed Ryan calls this the "mission of service" trait.

Then, you must have been a successful CEO or company leader. To have a high level of empathy for the person in the corner office, the corner office had to be yours.

You must be an excellent listener with the ability to ask the right questions.

You must have a high level of emotional intelligence.

Great CEO Group Leaders also have an "edge." What does that mean? Great CEO Group Leaders are masters of the fierce conversation. They will tell you what you need to hear, not what you want to hear. They have the guts to tell you the truth. In the words of Susan Scott, they have the *"courage to interrogate reality."* Why? Because they genuinely stand for your success. They genuinely care about you. They are in your corner unconditionally for the rest of their lives.

Jan Dowding is an outstanding CEO Group Leader. She cares deeply. As the former president and CEO of De Lage Landen Financial Services Canada Inc., Jan knows how to run successful companies. Says Jan, *"When I look back on my career, what I am most proud of is the impact I had on people. That satisfaction is far more lasting than the numbers at the bottom of the P&L. Seeing that somehow I helped make a difference in someone's life is fulfilling."*

Another outstanding CEO Group Leader is John Grainger, the past-president and CEO of Laidlaw Inc., a widely held public company with operating revenues of $3.5 billion and in excess of 80,000 employees. Most recently, John was president and CEO of National Truck Leasing System and NationaLease Purchasing Corp.. He feels that mentoring CEOs is a natural progression for some CEOs:

Being a guy who has always been interested in a variety of businesses, the mentoring opportunity was ideal for me. I like moving from one set of circumstances to the next. I enjoy the varied psychological challenges, the strategic challenges, and the interpersonal challenges of multiple business situations.

As a CEO Group Leader, I am inspired by the CEOs who

are eager to learn. I don't give a lot of advice, but I ask lots of questions. I help CEOs explore their thoughts and consider all the alternatives and the repercussions of whatever it is that they are considering. I no longer have the desire to be the "Wise Sage on the Stage" but am comfortable in my role of "Guide on the Side."

"You do a lot of listening," says Rick McClelland, the former CEO, chairman of the board, and director of Dynamex Inc. *"As a CEO Group Leader you come to understand who the CEOs really are, what their business is all about, what their strategic priorities are, what their motivations are behind their strategic priorities, and what areas they want to work on. You have to listen carefully. Listen, listen, listen!"*

"I undoubtedly feel better every time I leave a CEO group meeting. The others in my Group always help me gain perspective and get me back on track. We all have different backgrounds and we all have our specialties so they sort of help me think a little bit differently. Often it's that different perspective that can be the game changer."

~ Rick Morris, CEO, Construction Specialties Co.

Can you imagine having one of these outstanding people as your sounding board? Asking the tough questions; telling you the truth; holding your feet to the fire on what is important to you, your family, and your company.

YOUR CEO PEER GROUP

The highest performing CEO peer groups have 14 to 16 non-competing CEOs who meet every month for five hours to significantly improve the success and lives of every CEO around the table by giving each other candid, honest, caring feedback. They check each other's backswing. They have each other's back. They hold each other accountable for achieving what they said they would achieve.

Here is a typical profile of a CEO peer group; the CEO brain power at the table standing for your success:

In your CEO peer group there is 100 years of university education including MBAs, the arts, accounting and law degrees, engineering, and doctorates.

There is a combined business experience of 400 years.

Ten of the CEOs own their own business of which six of them are the founders.

Six of the CEOs are leading the business for the shareholders.

The total annual revenue for these businesses is over $2 billion.

They employ over 5,000 people.

These 5,000 people represent family members of over 20,000.

These CEOs stand for your success!

You meet with them every month to discuss the biggest opportunities and challenges around the table and stand for each other's success. Your role is to arrive at each meeting prepared to participate, listen, ask smart questions, act on the group's advice, and help the other CEOs in the Group succeed.

No need to be lonely—connect. Join a CEO peer group and gain a CEO Group Leader as a mentor.

Your stock will go up.

CEO Action Items to Connect with Other CEOs

1. Join a CEO peer group
2. Ensure that you have an experienced CEO as a mentor
3. Be curious and ask smart questions
4. Hone your listening skills
5. Stay Hungry and Stay Learning

Chapter Eight

An Open Letter
to a New CEO

"I am the fourth generation running this family business. My mother had led the Marketing/HR/Interior Design aspects and my father, the Sales and Operations side. They built it up to a fantastic point, and basically took the business as far as they could. I wanted to take it beyond that stage, but realized that I did not have all the experience and knowledge I needed to do so. I was warmly welcomed and fit right into my CEO peer group, although I went there not knowing what to expect. Right away I felt that I had found a place where I belonged. It felt as if I had been taken under the wing by some experienced folks. It was a great feeling. Perhaps it seems hokey but I had felt so isolated in the business, not really knowing if I was making all the right decisions, thinking about the bottom line, and looking for insights with lots of the questions.

Early on, in my peer group meeting, I was asked to present my company's KPIs. The group challenged me and made me aware that I needed more than a couple of historical reference points to run the business. "You can't make good decisions and you can't run your company blind," I learned. Because of them standing for my success, openly sharing their experiences, and generously providing me frank, quality, and timely feedback, I began to feel that I had a board of advisors watching out for me, walking beside me and who, in many ways, had my back.

I have come to realize that the company will grow as fast as I and the employees grow. In the past two years, we have gone on a tremendous personal and corporate growth spurt; coming solidly out of the recession and setting us up for accelerated growth in the future. We had to make many difficult decisions and choices, and then implement significant change within the company. It has not been easy, but necessary.

I received a tremendous amount of coaching from my CEO peer group when the business was temporarily put into special loans, or "corporate restructuring," as the bank called it. I am happy to say that we came out of that with flying colors, and decided to change banks. In year one, we brought our breakeven point down by $18 million and structured Mayhew for sustainable growth.

Internally, I made some fairly significant organizational changes that were challenging to execute but overdue for some time. My CEO peer group gave me the tools, courage, and support I needed to follow through on these changes. As a result, I now have a high-performing executive team whom I trust and know I can count on, and Mayhew has become a performance-based culture where quality work and commitment is recognized and rewarded.

It is a completely different way of looking at the business, and a lot more discipline and governance comes into play. Something fun that I learned at my first peer group meeting is, "Volume is vanity, Profit is sanity," and to this day my people hear me saying it over and over around the building, and are probably sick of hearing me, but I keep saying it. They understand it and that is exciting to me.

I think the time spent as a CEO or president to improve your decision making is an investment in yourself, and a gift to the organization that just keeps on giving."

Marcia Mayhew, CEO, Mayhew & Associates

Congratulations! You are now the CEO; with all the rights, privileges, and obligations that come with your new responsibilities. You are embarking on the most exciting business journey of your life!

You are now the person who will decide where to take the company. Your vision of the future will set everything else in motion.

Your behavior will have a huge impact on people.

You now have the opportunity to significantly improve the success and lives of all around you, and their families.

You now have an opportunity to learn more than you have ever learned to this point in your business life—about yourself, about those around you, and about your business. Stay thirsty for learning.

Ask yourself these three questions:

1. If I could have one decision back that I made in the past year, which one is it and why do I want it back?

2. What are the two biggest strategic decisions I have to make in the next year to take this company where I want to take it?

3. What is the number one thing I must get better at as the leader of this company to take it where I want to take it?

Your answers will help keep you focused on the things that will make you a Great CEO.

Watch your "emotional wake." Every time you interact with someone, enter a room, choose to not enter a room, ask a question, or make a joke—it will mean something to everyone around you. Make your emotional wake a positive one.

Continue to work on the key emotional intelligence skills for leaders: empathy, self-regard, self-awareness, assertiveness, and social skills. Great CEOs are highly motivated to hone these skills and work hard to keep them sharp.

Keep your eyes on the horizon. Create a passionate vision for your company and use the right tools to communicate that vision across your organization.

You will decide who will be on your team. You will decide who gets to share this exciting journey with you. Don't settle for less than the best in each position. These are the people who will determine your quality of life. If you don't surround yourself with the best, you will not achieve your vision. It simply cannot be done.

Decide on who the A players are going to be and then do the heavy lifting to ensure they become an A team. This team will determine whether or not you hit the ball out of the park with your financial results, if you will have the time to work on the business and not get buried in it, and, it will determine whether or not you will have quality time with those you love.

Don't forget to take the time to celebrate your team's successes. Recognition of a person's accomplishments and personal milestones is a great way to keep a winning team and build a winning company.

Take the time to privately celebrate your own successes as well.

Hold yourself and your team accountable for getting things done. It is critical for your team to put the numbers on the board. Hit the targets.

Hold people accountable to achieve the necessary results and have the courage to hold their feet to the fire. Have the fierce conversations when needed.

Understand the numbers for your business! This is critical. Get a top-notch financial dashboard that tells you where you are with your key performance indicators every day. Make sure that you know the leading indicators that will drive the performance of your company. Watch them like a hawk. Don't abdicate or delegate these key indicators. You have to own them. Understand them.

Remember that work–life balance means different things to different people. As a new CEO, you are on a very steep learning curve. Balance will be tough for a few months as you try to drink from a fire hose all the new things coming at you. There will be a lineup at your door. Keep things in perspective.

Do not be afraid to seek honest feedback. This is the secret sauce for Great CEOs. And the best place to get honest, candid, feedback is from non-competing peers and a mentor who is independent of your company.

Join a CEO peer group and take it seriously. Don't miss a meeting. Being with other CEOs who care about you will propel you to the top of every mountain you climb for the rest of your career. They will help you make wise choices on your biggest, most critical, decisions.

Your CEO Group Leader should stand unconditionally for your success and be in your corner for the rest of their life. Make sure they have strong business experience. This is essential if they are to be an effective sounding board for you. Make sure they are an outstanding listener and have the courage to ask you the tough questions that nobody else will ask you.

It can be lonely at the top. Your CEO peer group and Group Leader will take your loneliness away.

Stay hungry. Stay learning. Stay connected.

Enjoy the journey!

All the very best,

John Wilson
Founder and CEO
CEO Global Network Inc.
www.ceoglobalnetwork.com

Chapter Nine

An Open Letter
to a Veteran CEO

"I had been retired for almost three years, I was doing noth-ing and I was very determined that I was not going to sit on public or private boards. I had done a lot of that and didn't want to do that any longer, and I did not want to be an exec-utive-at-large, or without portfolio as a consultant. And I'm not a not-for-profit guy, I'm not an avid fund-raiser, I don't like asking people for money, and I'm not good at it.

I have always been very interested in a variety of businesses and had a personal need to do something of value to keep my hand in the business community about a week each month.

As a leader and executive I had supervised and helped de-velop multiple managers for many years. The thought of stay-ing involved with executives and mentoring people was natural for me. The challenges of heading up a public company, the fi-nancing, the analysts, and the stock markets are special. I felt I had something to offer these good folks. In smaller companies they often do not have anyone that has been there, done that, or can challenge their thinking and viewpoints from that perspective.

The safety of talking about issues to a mentor or a peer group in a confidential and unbiased way is appealing. They know it's not going to get back to their organization; it's a safe discussion. In all my executive roles and years, I never had that kind of opportunity, as I always had those "safe" conversations with myself, which may not have always been the best thing!

I have witnessed that it doesn't have to be a huge company to get yourself wound up, stressed and stretched out, and commonly working 80 hours a week. Even more so, small companies, or entrepreneurial businesses can do that to you in a heartbeat because "you're it," and thus if you're not going to do it, it's not going to get done. Often entrepreneurs try to do everything themselves, across all the layers in a business.

It is hard to do and sustain.

I am inspired by executives who are eager to learn. I like to be involved and also learn from them and to see what's new. I don't give a lot of advice, but I ask an awful lot of questions. I try to help people explore their thoughts; consider the alternatives and the repercussions of whatever they want to do."

John Grainger, Group Leader, CEO Global Network and past-President and CEO of Laidlaw Inc.

Have you reached a stage in your career where you have achieved balance, have a solid A team in place, and no longer need to spend as much time at the helm?

Perhaps you have stepped back from, or sold your company, but know that you still have value to add to the business community.

Maybe you have moved on from the corner office and are looking for a meaningful way to stay engaged in business.

Congratulations on now being in a position to pursue new opportunities and learn from new experiences!

You have spent your entire career developing and nurturing people, helping them grow and realize their potential. You have derived great satisfaction in mentoring other people over the decades.

Chances are you are still looking for something meaningful to do. You have had a life full of stimulation, travel, and challenges, and now find that you want to help other CEOs succeed.

You may have initially charged at the golf course, but after playing several times a week for a few months, are now looking for other challenges.

I want to let you know that the knowledge you have gained from successfully building your business career would be of great value to other CEOs who need someone who has "been in the fire" as their mentor.

Do you remember when you were a less-experienced CEO? It is lonely at the top! Mentoring CEOs is an opportunity to reduce their feeling of loneliness. Be their sounding board, their confidant. They will discuss things with you they can't discuss with anyone else in the world.

For the right veteran CEOs, being a CEO Group Leader will be the most fulfilling role of their career!

It builds energy, knowledge, courage.

It will take you places you never knew you could go and never knew you were capable of going.

If you have the right stuff you will love it!

Ask yourself:

Can you be the "guide on the side" rather than the "sage on the stage"?

Do you have a high level of business acumen, a solid depth and breadth of business experience, empathy, and the "mission of service" gene?

Do you have a passion to help other CEOs succeed? Can you stand for their success?

Are you an outstanding listener and able to hear between the lines?

Do you have the courage to interrogate reality and ask the tough questions?

Do you know when to speak and when to let the silence do the heavy lifting?

> Are you prepared to give unconditional support
> and not be judgmental?

I have had over 4,000 one-to-one meetings with CEOs, and have learned something from each one of them. The learning just never stops.

It is noble work—helping the few who influence so many, helping those who are building strong companies, creating great places to work, and contributing to the growth of the economies in their communities and countries.

You will gain so much more from the CEOs you are mentoring than you will ever give. You will learn so much about business and life. You will learn so much about yourself!

Let me know if you would like to learn more about becoming a CEO Group Leader.

I would be pleased to connect with you and help you decide if it is the right next step for you.

All the very best,

John Wilson
Founder and CEO
CEO Global Network Inc.
www.ceoglobalnetwork.com

CEO Action Items
Checklist

Get to Know Yourself

- ☐ Read *Primal Leadership* by Daniel Goleman
- ☐ Read *The EQ Edge* by Steven J. Stein, PhD, and Howard E. Book, MD
- ☐ Complete an Emotional Intelligence Self-Assessment (EQ-i)
- ☐ Find your "Carolyn Robertson" to help you establish your EI Development priority and develop a plan for improvement
- ☐ Solicit honest feedback on your progress

Create and Communicate an Inspiring Vision

- ☐ Write an inspiring vision for your company

Get alignment on your vision across your organization:

- ☐ Read *Mastering the Rockefeller Habits* by Verne Harnish and create a One-Page Strategic Plan
- ☐ Read *CEO Tools* by Kraig Kramers and create a One Page Business Plan
- ☐ Conduct monthly one-to-one meetings with each of your direct reports

Communicate your vision across your organization:

- ☐ Walk the Four Corners
- ☐ Repeat the message and tell the story

Build an A Team

- ☐ Read the book *Topgrading* by Bradford D. Smart
- ☐ Create a Talent Audit for your organization
- ☐ Define the benchmark behavior traits of top performers within your organization
- ☐ Start a Talent File
- ☐ Read Patrick Lencioni's *The Five Dysfunctions of a Team*
- ☐ Complete Patrick Lencioni's Team Assessment and work on the biggest gap
- ☐ Recognize at least one of your team players this week and every week for the rest of your career
- ☐ Create a succession plan

Create a Culture of Accountability

- ☐ Read Patrick Lencioni's *The Five Temptations of a CEO*
- ☐ Read Patrick Lencioni's *Death by Meeting*
- ☐ Implement Patrick Lencioni's Four Meetings
- ☐ Define and communicate goals and responsibilities across your organization

Dramatically improve your company's performance

- ☐ Use the Hartman KPI Template and Kraig Kramers' T12M charts as a financial dashboard
- ☐ Complete a CEO Report Card

☐ Complete a Leadership 360 and work on the biggest gap

☐ Implement a Behavior Benchmark program for hiring

☐ Read *Catalytic Coaching: The End of the Performance Review* by Gary Markle

☐ Implement Catalytic Coaching

☐ Implement Quarterly Priorities Management to keep you and your team focused on the right stuff

☐ Read Susan Scott's *Fierce Conversations*—and have the one you are avoiding

Achieve Your Perfect Balance

☐ Ensure that you have an A team in place (see Chapter 3)

☐ Work *on* your business more, and *in it* less

☐ Answer the question: What do you want from your life?

☐ Take time out to "let the big ideas in" and determine your life's purpose

☐ Based on your life's purpose, identify your Perfect Balance role model

☐ Develop a plan to achieve your life's purpose

☐ Think Dale Armstrong and Derek Bullen— execute your plan to achieve your life's purpose

Become Connected

- ☐ Join a CEO peer group
- ☐ Ensure that you have an experienced CEO as a mentor
- ☐ Be curious and ask smart questions
- ☐ Hone your listening skills
- ☐ Stay Hungry and Stay Learning

REMEMBER THE SEVEN IMPERATIVES:

Be connected;
accept the support and knowledge of your peers

Emotional Intelligence;
understand yourself and others

Great tools;
use the best information to make quality decisions

Right people;
find, keep, and inspire them

Equilibrium;
identify and create your perfect **work–life balance**

Ability to inspire;
generate and communicate a great vision

Take responsibility;
be accountable and get things done!

Appendix
Worksheets and Samples

Catalytic Coaching Input Sheet, Page 1

COACHING INPUT SHEET

Name: _____   Job Title: _____

Department/Division: _____   Time in Position: _____

Date: _____   Time w/ Coach: _____

1. WHAT I'VE DONE FOR *THE COMPANY* LATELY

My Accomplishments – What I Set Out To Do and Did

-
-
-
-

My Disappointments – What I Set Out To Do and Didn't

-
-
-
-

2. WHAT I'VE DONE FOR *MYSELF* LATELY

My Own Personal Growth

- NEW SKILLS (COMPETENCIES) I'VE ACQUIRED:

- IMPORTANT EXPERIENCE I'VE GAINED:

- RELATIONSHIPS I'VE BUILT THAT AID MY PRODUCTIVE CAPACITY:

Catalytic Coaching Input Sheet, Page 2

Page 2

3. WHAT I'D LIKE TO BE WHEN I GROW UP

My Career Aspirations

- WHAT I WOULD LIKE TO BE/DO IN THE NEXT <u>YEAR OR TWO:</u>

- WHAT I WOULD LIKE TO BE /DO IN THE NEXT <u>FIVE YEARS:</u>

- WHAT I ULTIMATELY <u>ASPIRE</u> TO BE/DO:

4. OTHER IMPORTANT THINGS I'D LIKE YOU TO KNOW AS MY COACH

My Situation/Professional Questions

- MY MOBILITY ISSUES/ DESIRES/CONSTRAINTS:

- MY PAY OR BENEFITS ISSUES:

- MY OTHER QUESTIONS/CONCERNS/ISSUES:

Name: _____   Date Submitted: _____

Coach: _____   Date of Discussion: _____

Catalytic Coaching Worksheet, Page 1

CATALYTIC COACHING WORKSHEET

Name: _____ Job Title: _____

Department/Division: _____ Time in Position: _____

Date: _____ Time w/ Coach: _____

STRENGTHS

- Ability to get results and achieve sales results of 103% of plan
- Technical expertise in new product development contributing $500,000 profit
- Leading team productivity to a record level of 110% over last year
- Developing direct reports to take on increased responsibility
- Continually improving skills and value to company such as completed finance and accounting training.

AREAS FOR IMPROVEMENT

Performance Impacting	Potential Enhancing	Job Threatening	
X			• Develop a strategic plan for Canadian business
	X		• Increase knowledge of Balance Sheet and Income Statement
	X		• Focus on priorities – increased discernment on highest and best use of time
		X	• Reduce level of employee turnover in Alberta and B.C. regions

DEVELOPMENT RECOMMENDATIONS

- Improve communication skills with employees
- Develop planning skills
- Increase financial knowledge of our business
- Management of priorities

Coach: _____ Human Resources: _____

Reviewing Manager/s: _____ Associate: _____

Catalytic Coaching Worksheet, Page 2

DEFINITION OF TERMS

STRENGTHS

Characteristics or attributes regarded as noteworthy in a positive manner. Strengths should be clearly tailored and specific to each individual.

AREAS FOR IMPROVEMENT (AFI)

Characteristics or attributes regarded as places to concentrate improvement efforts to achieve optimum benefit to the individual and Company. AFIs do not necessarily imply deficiency. In keeping with our theme of continuous improvement, everyone has numerous areas in which to get better. Selecting 3 to 5 AFIs per individual per counseling period helps focus attention on areas the supervisor perceives to be of highest priority. Each AFI should be classified in one of the following ways, based on the *primary* message that management is trying to convey. If an AFI is considered to have two equally weighted messages, two boxes can be checked.

- Performance Impacting
  This AFI describes performance that, if improved measurably, may result in an increased contribution in the *current* assignment. It does not necessarily imply deficiency. At minimum, however, it represents an opportunity to enhance an associate's personal impact or organizational productivity. Importance for improvement in this area may range from helpful to important.

- Potential Enhancing
  This AFI describes performance that, if improved measurably, may result in increasing an employee's potential for advancement to higher levels within the corporation. Improvement in this area does not necessitate promotion so much as it enhances the likelihood of being competitive for one, should the opportunity exist.

- Job Threatening
  This AFI, describes performance below an acceptable level. If an employee does not improve this aspect of his/her work significantly for a sustained period of time, it may result in his/her removal from the current job assignment through transfer, demotion or termination of employment. Importance for improving this area requires immediate attention.

DEVELOPMENT RECOMMENDATIONS

This section contains suggested activities to help the employee improve in the areas noted above. Development recommendations can include training or classroom instruction, mentoring or coaching, or exposure to different work experiences. It can also include regularly scheduled follow-up coaching, counseling and feedback sessions.

Catalytic Coaching Personal Development Plan

PERSONAL DEVELOPMENT PLAN

Name: _____   Job Title: _____

Department/Division: _____   Time in Position: _____

Date: _____   Time w/ Coach: _____

| **IMPROVEMENT GOALS** | This section sets forth an action plan for my personal development and itemizes steps I will take to address no more than four Areas for Improvement from my Performance Coaching Worksheet or from growth needs highlighted by the other developmental processes. |

Goal 1 _____
-
-

Goal 2 _____
-
-

Goal 3 _____
-
-

Goal 4 _____
-
-

| **STRENGTHS** | This section is an attempt to help me capitalize on my strengths and contains a goal based on one of my strengths as listed in my *Catalytic Coaching Worksheet* and/or other developmental feedback. |

Goal 5 _____
-
-

Associate: _____   Date Submitted _____

Coach: _____   Date Approved: _____

© 2003 by Energage Inc. All rights Reserved.
Reprinted with permission.

Sample MPR Feedback

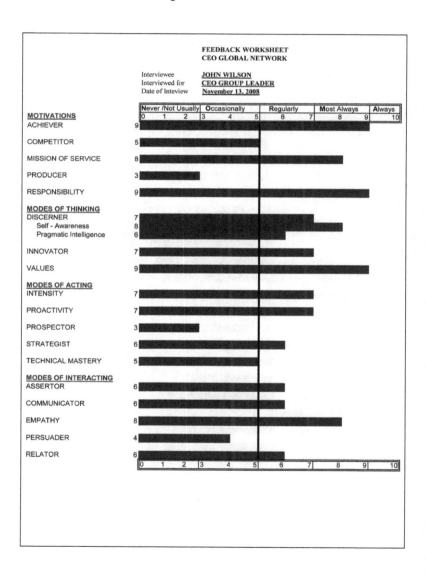

Sample EQ-i Results

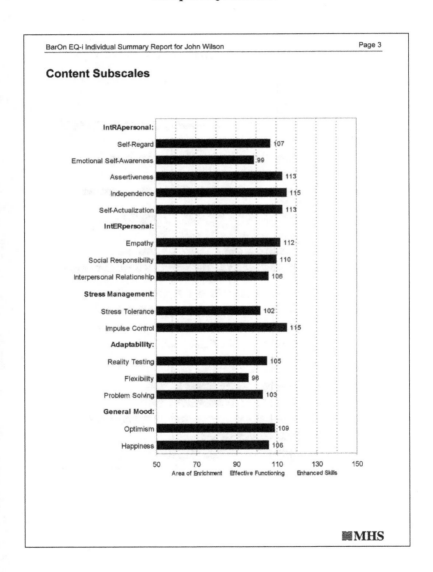

Content Subscales

IntRApersonal:
- Self-Regard — 107
- Emotional Self-Awareness — 99
- Assertiveness — 113
- Independence — 115
- Self-Actualization — 113

IntERpersonal:
- Empathy — 112
- Social Responsibility — 110
- Interpersonal Relationship — 106

Stress Management:
- Stress Tolerance — 102
- Impulse Control — 115

Adaptability:
- Reality Testing — 105
- Flexibility — 96
- Problem Solving — 103

General Mood:
- Optimism — 109
- Happiness — 106

50   70   90   110   130   150

Area of Enrichment   Effective Functioning   Enhanced Skills

MHS

LPI Questionnaire (Kouzes and Posner)

Leadership Practices Inventory

The rating scale runs from 1 to 10
1 - Almost Never	6 - Sometimes
2 - Rarely	7 - Fairly Often
3 - Seldom	8 - Usually
4 - Once in a While	9 - Very Frequently
5 - Occasionally	10 - Almost Always

Leadership Behaviors Ranking

This page shows the ranking, from most frequent ("high") to least frequent ("low") of all 30 leadership behaviors based on the average Observers' score. A horizontal line separates the 10 least frequent behaviors from the others. An asterisk (*) next to the Observer score indicates that the Observer score and the Self score differ by more than plus or minus 1.5.

High

	Practice	Self	Observers
17. Shows others how their interests can be realized	Inspire	5	8.3*
13. Searches outside organization for innovative ways to improve	Challenge	4	7.8*
9. Actively listens to diverse points of view	Enable	4	7.7*
14. Treats people with dignity and respect	Enable	5	7.5*
30. Gives team members appreciation and support	Encourage	4	7.5*
26. Is clear about his/her philosophy of leadership	Model	4	7.5*
3. Seeks challenging opportunities to test skills	Challenge	4	7.5*
18. Asks "What can we learn?"	Challenge	8	7.3
27. Speaks with conviction about meaning of work	Inspire	5	7.3*
20. Recognizes people for commitment to shared values	Encourage	9	7.2*
19. Supports decisions other people make	Enable	4	7.2*
28. Experiments and takes risks	Challenge	6	7.0
16. Asks for feedback on how his/her actions affect people's performance	Model	6	7.0
23. Makes certain that goals, plans, and milestones are set	Challenge	4	7.0*
4. Develops cooperative relationships	Enable	8	6.8
15. Creatively rewards people for their contributions	Encourage	4	6.8*
6. Makes certain that people adhere to agreed-on standards	Model	8	6.5*
29. Ensures that people grow in their jobs	Enable	7	6.5
12. Appeals to others to share dream of the future	Inspire	2	6.5*
7. Describes a compelling image of the future	Inspire	7	6.3
24. Gives people choice about how to do their work	Enable	6	6.3
10. Expresses confidence in people's abilities	Encourage	5	6.2
5. Praises people for a job well done	Encourage	9	6.0*
25. Finds ways to celebrate accomplishments	Encourage	7	5.8
22. Paints "big picture" of group aspirations	Inspire	5	5.8
8. Challenges people to try new approaches	Challenge	4	5.8*
21. Builds consensus around organization's values	Model	7	5.3*
2. Talks about future trends influencing our work	Inspire	7	5.3*
1. Sets a personal example of what is expected	Model	6	5.2
11. Follows through on promises and commitments	Model	8	4.5*

Low   *Difference between Observer's and Self rating was greater than 1.5

3

Acknowledgments

Twelve years ago, I attended a CEO breakfast meeting with 50 CEOs I had never met. The meeting was called to order and everyone was asked to find a seat. I searched the room for an available chair and made my way over to a table.

I introduced myself, and the man on my right replied, "Good morning, John. I'm Rick Fitzgerald." At the time, I had no idea how fortunate I was that the chair beside Rick had not yet been taken.

Rick has had a huge impact on my life.

He is the reason this book has been written and I can't imagine a more appropriate person to have put the ball in play for *Great CEOs and How They Are Made*. Rick is a Great CEO and a role model for each of the Seven Imperatives.

It was at a CEO Global Network Advisory Board meeting almost three years ago that Rick first suggested we write a book. A book about the lessons learned from the Great CEOs we have had the opportunity to work with over so many years. In his wisdom, Rick believed that this book would be of great value for CEOs and executives globally. It would help them significantly improve their business success, their lives, and the lives of those they love.

Rick led the charge to get this book written and put considerable focus and energy into personally interviewing each of the CEOs you will learn from in this book, as well as many other CEOs whose feedback helped shape the book both in content and in spirit. It was a huge undertaking and Rick took it on with enthusiasm and passion.

Rick is also a great friend. I know he will be in my corner unconditionally for the rest of my life. He truly stands for my success. He encourages me to live in a bigger world. He is a man of inspiring vision. He is a person you definitely want on your team, no matter what business you are in, or what sport you are playing.

Thank you, Rick. I had no idea how much my life would change when I took that seat at your table.

In September 2010, Rick introduced me to Susan Hart.

"John, I would like you to meet Susan. Susan helps people turn book ideas into realities. She gets things done." Susan's business card said project management. She is a great project manager, and more.

I doubt you would be reading this book if it hadn't been for Susan. I don't think we would have got the ball over the goal line without Susan carrying the ball. Susan got it done and in such a nice way. She handled the hundreds of details that went into getting this book in your hands. She gently guided us every step along the way. And she did it all with grace and a wonderful sense of humor.

Thank you, Susan.

Another person who has been with me every step of the way is Carolyn Robertson. Anyone who knows me knows how much I respect and admire Carolyn. I hold her in very high esteem. She has been my confidant and mentor during a very important and exciting time in my life. Carolyn helps me in many ways, not the least of which is helping me get to know myself better. She has also encouraged me to "live in a bigger world" and become all I can be. You will have an opportunity to learn some major lessons from Carolyn in this book. Thank you Carolyn for sharing these lessons and thank you for everything you have taught me.

I also want to thank Hugh MacKinnon, Chairman & CEO of Bennett Jones LLP for writing the Foreword. Hugh is without question one of the highest-performing CEOs in the world, so his thoughts on *Great CEOs and How They Are Made* are coming from a man with the highest level of credibility. Thank you for all your help and guidance along the way, Hugh.

I also want to acknowledge all of the CEOs you will learn from in these pages. They are without question some of the best and brightest, and are each making a significant difference in their companies and in the lives and communities they touch. They are truly Great CEOs. I appreciate their willingness to allow me to share their stories with you. I have learned so much from them and you will as well. My sincerest thanks to Anne Martin, Bill Kooy, Boris Bratuhin, Chris Gower, Christie Henderson, Cliff Sarjeant, Dale Armstrong, David Dobbin, Dean Martin, Frank Geier, George Sittlinger, Grant Heggie, Helen Pike,

Ian Collins, Jamie Moody, Jan Dowding, Jim Greenwood, John Grainger, John Piercy, Lisa MacNeil, Marcia Mayhew, Michael Burrows, Michael Grochmal, Michael Reinders, Naseem Somani, Paul Rockett, Rick McClelland, Rick Morris, Roger Grochmal , Shelley Wishart, Steve Gallant, Steve Hartman, and William Tharp.

As well, my deepest appreciation to the CEOs and executives (including Glenn Laverty, Graham Clark, Chris Powell and Dale Findlay) who provided comments on their CEO Global Network experience for inclusion at the front of the book.

I also want to acknowledge and thank the outstanding business thinkers and best-selling business authors who have made significant contributions to my learning. Their teachings have changed the lives of so many CEOs and executives. I thank them for letting me include some of their thoughts and lessons in this book. Thank you to Barry Posner, Bradford Smart, Daniel Goleman, Derek Bullen, Ed Ryan, Gary Markle, Jack Daly, Jim Kouzes, Kraig Kramers, Marshall Goldsmith, Michael McKinney, Patrick Lencioni, Saj-nicole Joni, Susan Scott, Verne Harnish, and John Wiley & Sons, Inc.

And thank you to Kevin Morris, a very intelligent young man with a bright future. Kevin played an important role in the early stages of the book's development, contributing many fresh and innovative ideas to our discussions.

This book has been almost three years in the making. This has meant that some quality time with my wife Lynne, and our daughter Jen, has been sacrificed along the way. Thank you both so much for your understanding on those long days when I had the *Please do not disturb* sign on my door and only Ollie, our 17 year old shih tzu, was allowed in. Your support and consideration during this time was deeply appreciated.

Index

loneliness. *See* connecting with other CEOs

M

MacNeil, Lisa, 129
managing partners. *See* Great CEOs
Maple Lodge Farms, 33–34, 60–61. *See* also Burrows, Michael
Maple Reinders Group Ltd., 23. *See also* Reinders, Mike
Maracle Press Ltd. *See* Sittlinger, George
marketing, and CEO Report Card, 100
Marketing Personnel Research Inc. *See* Ryan, Ed
Markle, Garold, 108–11
Catalytic Coaching, 109, 117
Martin, Anne, 135, 138
Martin, Dean, 121–24
Mastering the Rockefeller Habits (Harnish), 37, 42
Mayhew, Marcia, 145–46, 150, 157–59
Mayhew & Associates, 146, 157, 158. *See also* Mayhew, Marcia
McCarthy, Dan, 76
McClelland, Rick, 93–94, 152
McDonald's Restaurants, 37
McKinney, Michael, 25–26
meetings. *See also* peer groups
to achieve alignment, 39–40
with direct reports, 39–40, 42
Four Meetings Method, 83–85, 87, 88

with management team, 34
one-on-one with VPs, 87
team-building and, 61
to work on self, 22
Melmart Distributors Inc., 121. *See also* Heggie, Grant; Martin, Dean
mentoring, 150–52, 165–69
mentors, 25, 139–40. *See also* CEO Group Leaders; connecting with other CEOs
MHS, 18, 184
Mobilicity. *See* Dobbin, David
Monthly Strategic meeting, 83, 84
Moody, Jamie, 78–79, 85–88, 144
Morris, Rick, 141–2, 152
motivation, 16, 106–7
Mountain Cable. *See* Piercy, John
Myers-Briggs Type Indicator, 60

N

NationaLease Purchasing Corp. *See* Grainger, John
National Truck Leasing System. *See* Grainger, John
NCI Canada Inc. *See* Sarjeant, Cliff
Nelson, Bob
1001 Ways to Recognize Employees, 67
1001 Ways to Reward Employees, 67
new CEOs, advice for, 160–63

O

OI Partners, 69–70
One Minute Manager, The
  (Blanchard), 66
One Page Business Plan, 38–39
One-Page Strategic Plan, 37–38,
  39, 42
*1001 Ways to Recognize
  Employees* (Nelson), 67
1001 Ways to Reward Employees
  (Nelson), 67
operations, and CEO Report
  Card, 100
optimism, and self-motivation,
  20
Orchard International Inc., 80.
  See also Wishart, Shelley
Oxygen Capital Corp.
  See Sittlinger, George

P

passion, 41–42, 49. *See also*
  inspiring others
PCL Constructors Canada Inc.,
  22. *See also* Gower, Chris
peer groups, 5
  accountability and, 78–80,
    82, 85, 88
  connecting with other CEOs,
    142–43, 153–54, 163
  qualities of, 139
  succession planning and,
    70–72
  success story, 75, 157–59
  typical profile of, 10–11,
    153–54
  value of, 139–40, 163

work-life balance and, 124,
  129, 166
performance management
  systems. *See also* key
    performance indicators
  Catalytic Coaching, 93,
    108–11, 178–82
  CEO Report Card, 98–101
Personal Development Plan.
  See Catalytic Coaching
personal growth, 2, 15, 128, 130
Piercy, John, 40–41
Pike, Helen, 80
players. *See* "A" players; average
  players
politics, and average players,
  49–50
popularity, 48, 50–51, 83.
  See also conflict
Posner, Barry, 103–4
  The Leadership Challenge,
    103, 185
presidents. *See* Great CEOs
Primal Leadership (Goleman),
  14, 21, 136
prioritizing, 38, 111–13
problem solving, 20
Profit$ Magazine, 126
promoting, 106
purpose, 38, 39. *See also*
  work-life balance

Q

quality of work, 77
Quarterly Off-site Review
  meeting, 83, 84–85, 86, 87
Quarterly Priorities
  Management, 111–13, 117

others; team-building;
tools; work-life balance
and the CEO peer group,
9–11
Shaw Communications. *See*
Piercy, John
Sherway Group, 21–22. *See also*
Rockett, Paul
S.i. Systems Ltd., 126, 130.
See also Bullen, Derek
Sittlinger, George, 75, 76
Smart, Bradford D., 46–47
on average players, 49–51
*Cost of Mis-hire Study
Results*, 52
Topgrading, 46–47, 51–52
Smith, Tom
Journey to the Emerald City,
77
social awareness, 19. *See also*
empathy
social skills, 16, 161
Somani, Naseem, 146
Southwest Airlines, 36.
See also Kelleher, Herb
speeches, inspiring, 30
Stein, Steven J., 18
emotional quotient
inventory (EQ-i), 17–21,
184
The EQ Edge, 18, 21
storytelling, 36–37, 42
strategic plans
key components of, 39
Kramers' One-Page Business
Plan and, 38–39, 42
Monthly Strategic Meeting,
83, 84

One-Page Strategic Plan,
37–38, 39, 42
Quarterly Off-site Review
meeting, 84–85, 86
Quarterly Priorities
Management, 111–13
sharing with employees,
38–39
stress management, 20
Succession (Goldsmith), 69
succession planning. *See also*
CEO Report Card
developing successors, 70–72
family-owned businesses
and, 70, 71–72
OI Partners' survey, 69–70
team-building and, 68–70,
73
success stories
accountability, 85–88
decision making, 157–59
emotional intelligence, 21–24
peer groups, 75, 157–59
tools and, 91
work-life balance, 126–28,
130

T

tactical goals, 87
Talent Audit, 53–54, 73
talent file, of "A" players, 55, 73
team-building, 45–73. *See also*
CEO Report Card;
confrontation
accountability and, 77
action items, 73, 173
assessment of team, 56–57, 73

Notes

Notes

Notes

Notes

Notes

Notes